The Great Peace March

The Great

A Peacewatch Edition

Peace March

An American Odyssey

by Franklin Folsom and Connie Fledderjohann

with Gerda Lawrence

OCEAN TREE BOOKS

Santa Fe, New Mexico • 1988

An Ocean Tree Books *Peacewatch Edition*
O C E A N   T R E E   B O O K S
Post Office Box 1295
Santa Fe, New Mexico 87504

The story of **The Great Peace March** is a complex one, involving hundreds of individuals. If any important fact was omitted or error inadvertently made, the authors express their sincere regret, and invite the reader to write them in care of the publisher.

Printed in the United States of America.
Peacewatch Editions editor, Richard Polese
Design & typesetting by *Desktop Personal Publishing*, Boulder, CO
Cover photograph by Dan Coogan.

International Standard Book Number: 0-943734-14-2

Library of Congress Cataloging in Publication data:

Folsom, Franklin, 1907–
    The Great Peace March: An American Odyssey / by Franklin Folsom
and Connie Fledderjohann with Gerda Lawrence.
    206p.   cm. — (A Peacewatch edition)
    Bibliography: p. 203
    ISBN 0-943734-14-2 : $10.95
    1. Antinuclear movement—United States.   I. Fledderjohann,
Connie, 1931–   II. Lawrence, Gerda.   III. Title.   IV. Series.
JX1974.7.F65 1988
327.1'74'0973—dc19   88-9947
                                                            CIP

Contents

Marchers...

Preface

Any small community can be worthy of a book and the Great Peace March for Global Nuclear Disarmament (the GPM)—also known as Peace City—was a small community. But it was also a community that came together around a big idea. It was a determined response to the greatest danger that humanity has ever had to face.

Peace City did not grow up at a crossroads or near a harbor or close to some natural resource, as often happens with settlements. Instead it was constantly on the move. Every day it advanced toward a goal that was both geographical and political. In many ways it was unique.

We hope that our story about the colorful trek of the GPM will attract readers who could only view it from afar, if at all. And because the GPM developed from an idea, we have tried to write something that will be useful to those who share that idea. We have written for the growing number of those who believe that nuclear disarmament is absolutely essential for human survival. And we have written at a time when the world peace movement sees clear evidence that citizen peace actions can get results. They helped create the climate which required the INF Treaty—the vital first step on the road toward total nuclear disarmament.

Finally this book tries to satisfy the desire that many Marchers from Peace City have expressed for a permanent record of something they helped to create. We hope these Marchers will find that our book is really about them, even when they do not find their names among the few that could be mentioned in our limited space.

Franklin Folsom
Boulder, Colorado
March, 1988

. . . . . .

Before the conclusion of the Great Peace March I realized that it would not be over for me when we reached Washington. I decided to retrace my steps across the country, this time by car, to interview people along the route about the effect of the March on them and on their communities. Before leaving on the second cross-country journey I had made plans with Franklin Folsom to combine our efforts on this book, which includes material I collected from Marchers, March supporters and onlookers during that four-and-a-half month trip.

Diversity, which was a hallmark of the Great Peace March, is reflected also in the viewpoints of the two authors of this book. While agreeing on most of what is included in this account, we encountered some differences based on our respective backgrounds and political and philosophical beliefs. Rather than choosing to avoid the areas of disagreement we have tried to present both points of view and still maintain a consistent account of the events.

Franklin, as a member of the Board of Directors and the City Council, served the March as an elected representative, and his experience and interest have inclined him to treat the governmental and political side of the GPM more extensively and differently than I chose to do. I, on the other hand, come from a background of teaching and psychology and have found the interpersonal relationships and human interest stories most appealing.

Also we have tried to understand the different points of view expressed by the Marchers. It is our hope that our joint efforts have resulted in a more complete picture of this historic event than either of us alone could have drawn.

The experience of collaborating with Franklin in this effort has been a wonderful learning opportunity for me. Both Franklin and his wife (and our editor), Mary Elting Folsom, have been generous, patient and understanding with me in my first attempt at a book.

Connie Fledderjohann
Boulder, Colorado
March, 1988

. . . . . .

As the March ended, it became increasingly important to me to document how we managed the daily business of living. How did we keep healthy, dispose of our waste, secure our equipment and keep it repaired, find campsites, educate ourselves to speak to people, take care of our children? To answer such questions I spoke to many Marchers who headed departments and worked at jobs. In Chapter IV, you will be reading what people told me or what I understood them to say. Had I talked with other Marchers I would most likely have received different descriptions of events and organizational structures.

What I hope to convey is a flavor of how systems and ways of doing things were invented and how they continued to evolve. To me it is an exciting flavor, untidy and pungent with an energy ranging from focused to frantic. But mostly it conveys the diversity of the March. That is what gave it its vitality and enabled it to reach many different kinds of people along its route. The diversity also gave us the opportunity to develop an understanding of and skills in cross-cultural consensual decision making, which are the skills needed to solve international problems non-violently.

A great many creative and dedicated people made the March across this land of ours happen. The March brought renewed hope and energy to peace groups. It also helped to connect many who continue to work for that which is our and our childrens' birthright: a life without the threat of nuclear annhilation and one in which eventually we will learn to live in peace with one another. *I wish you peace,*

Gerda Lawrence
Los Angeles, California
March, 1988

. . . . . .

The Great Peace March is a story of more than a thousand very diverse and determined people. Franklin Folsom, 80, writer, scholar and long-time activist; and Connie Fledderjohann, 57, teacher and psychotherapist, were just two of them. We were aided in our efforts by Gerda Lawrence whose interviews provide the stories and information in Chapter IV. We know there are many stories of the March—as many as there were Marchers. No doubt there were fascinating events, significant viewpoints and revealing incidents that should be included (but are not) in this book. We apologize, but we were only two among the multitude and our first jobs were to march and to serve. More about this unique American experience can be found in the Peace Collection of the Swarthmore College Library, back issues of *Peace City News*, current updates of the GPM's *Silver Thread*, in *Feet Across America* by Anne Macfarlane, in Cathy Zheutlin's film, *Just One Step (The Great Peace March)* and in the recollections of hundreds of thousands of Americans we met along the way, as well as in the memories and writing of Marchers, whose lives were forever changed by this commitment.

At the back of this book we list with sincere thanks those without whose help of one kind or another it could not have been written. To all who participated in the Great Peace March and to a world free of nuclear armaments, this book is dedicated.

F.F. & C.F.

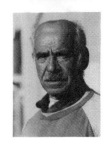

Introduction

In early 1986, 22-year-old Rick knew vaguely that nuclear war was a possibility, and he supposed that nuclear weapons were here to stay.

Rick had drifted aimlessly about, with no belief that life held much for him. And, like many others of his generation in America, he had tried to mask his feeling of emptiness by using drugs and alcohol. This supposedly all-American kid was a recovering addict when he heard of a way to fulfill one of the few dreams he had—a dream that had been with him since his days as a Boy Scout—to walk across the United States. He found that he could, in a drug-free and alcohol-free environment, join a large body of people who were going to walk all the way from Los Angeles to Washington, D.C.

These people would be protesting against nuclear arms. Rick had always regarded himself as too patriotic to be involved in protests, and he actually had little interest in the 50,000 nuclear weapons that now threatened all life on this planet. He certainly had no expectation that this venture on which he wanted to embark would help bring about any social changes.

Nine months later, when the Great Peace March was over, Rick realized that he had been through the greatest learning experience of his life. In Nevada he had walked not far from places where his government was conducting nuclear tests. In Utah he met people living downwind of the tests—people whose neighbors had developed cancer at five times the rate at which the disease appears in the rest of the population. In Colorado, he heard Geiger counters click above sidewalks and in buildings made from the tailings of uranium mines. In Ohio and Pennsylvania he saw steelworkers locked out of mills whose owners had found more profitable ways of making money. In Harlem, Rick mingled with people who suffered from unemployment. He suspected that this joblessness resulted, at least in part, from factories producing things that destroy instead of producing things that could create wealth.

During the Great Peace March, Rick's patriotism expanded. It became a patriotism that included the entire planet; now his life is as full of purpose as it had been empty.

Rick is a real person—his name is Rick Life and he lives in Colorado Springs. After crossing the country, he became very busy lecturing on the nuclear arms race, and he is only one of hundreds whom the Great Peace March launched into intensified activity against nuclear weapons.

The first deployed nuclear device—then called an atomic bomb—killed 100,000 people when it was dropped on Hiroshima on August 6, 1945. The Soviet Union, fearful that it might be a target for such bombs in the future, quickly developed a nuclear weapon of its own. The US followed with Edward Teller's thermonuclear (hydrogen) bomb, which was soon followed by the Soviets' development of their own H-bomb. For the next four decades, a fierce arms race escalated. Every time the United States added a new type of nuclear weapon or delivery system to its arsenal, the Soviet Union developed a similar weapon, and more nations—Britain, France, China, India, Israel—joined the lethal competition. By 1985, some 50,000 of these instruments of mass destruction had come out of the laboratories and factories of the great industrial powers. And many thousands of these doomsday devices are more powerful than the bombs that leveled Hiroshima and Nagasaki.

Scientists in the 1960s began to use a new word—overkill. The weapons they had developed could destroy all humanity many times over, and these weapons can be fired by accident as well as on purpose. If a handful of human beings should survive such an accidental or insane or evil unleashing of even a fraction of such weapons, a new horror would envelop them: a nuclear winter that would radically alter the environment on which all life depends.

Despite the fact that nuclear weapons, if used, would bring humanity to the end of its road, production has continued relentlessly in the United States and the USSR. And now, Pakistan, South Africa and possibly other countries may have them as well.

Over the years, peace organizations in the United States, Britain, West Germany, Japan, the Netherlands, New Zealand, the Soviet Union and other countries had been very active, trying to restore hope to the world, but their efforts had not slowed the arms race. Could an effort of a new kind make a difference? In the spring of 1986, more than a thousand people gathered in Los Angeles to begin a long walk across the United States in a new type of demonstration against nuclear weapons. A few in this throng were seasoned activists who had been taking part in anti-nuclear demonstrations and actions for years. And some, like Rick, were attracted by the challenge and adventure that a transcontinental walk would surely entail. Others, who were neither activists nor even lovers of adventure, felt deeply that the arms race was out of hand, the politicians weren't doing much to stop it, and they simply *had* to take part.

Looking at the group as they prepared to leave Los Angeles one might have been tempted to laugh at the audacity of this conglomeration of people. They were young, old and inbetween, overweight, fit, unfit, smokers and non-smokers, vegetarians and junk food junkies, experienced hikers and obvious tenderfeet. They were going to walk across the country—together?

The fact that more than a third of that original group—young and old and inbetween—did cross the continent on foot is now history, a history we will try to relate in this book. How much those who marched added to the struggle to turn the arms race around we leave to the reader to decide.

Chapter I

The Great Response

March 1   :   Los Angeles, CA
March 3   :   Claremont, CA
March 5-6   :   Glen Helen, CA
March 8-9   :   Victorville, CA
March 10-15 :   Stoddard Wells near Barstow
March 16-28 :   BMX track in Barstow, CA

As the Great Peace March neared Washington, Kathleen Hendrix, a *Los Angeles Times* staff writer who had covered the March from the beginning, summarized its origins in these words:

> The vision: That on March 1, 1986, 5,000 Americans would set out on foot from Los Angeles for Washington, walking across the country for global disarmament. They would reach some 65,000,000 Americans along the way, creating in them—and in the country and the world that watched—the moral and political climate necessary to bring about their goal.

> Corporate donors and sophisticated merchandising

would help finance the $20 million high-tech venture. Thousands would line the streets to welcome the marchers along the route and thousands more would visit the movable, solar-powered, mural festooned, environmentally friendly model community, Peace City. And, out there in the m.o.n.—the middle of nowhere—the townsfolk of America would be educated about the arms race by marchers and visiting experts, and be entertained by celebrities ranging from Hollywood's Establishment to its Brat Pack.

One hundred-thousand would cheer their send-off at a rock concert at the L.A. Coliseum. One million would join them on the outskirts of Washington on Nov. 14, and march into the capital with them at sunrise. Then, having compiled a computerized list of 10 million names gathered across the country, the sponsoring organization, PRO-Peace (People Reaching Out for Peace), would be ready to call for massive civil disobedience, and to take the march overseas, if those drastic steps seemed necessary—in the words of PRO-Peace founder David Mixner—"to bring those suckers down." *

A journey of a thousand miles begins with one step.

–Lao-Tse

The reality was something else, something more profoundly important than the glitzy parade that Mixner had dreamed up. But it would be a while before this would become apparent. From a diminished beginning on March 1, 1986, the PRO-Peace enterprise went downhill and continued to do so for ten days. Then something new and remarkable began. We will focus here on this new start and its surprising consequences.

But first a few facts about the initial debacle. David Mixner, 39, a partner in a Los Angeles public relations firm, had a background in Democratic politics. He said the inspiration for the March came from his seven-year-old niece who was afraid she would not grow up because of nuclear bombs. Mixner had the idea for PRO-Peace late in 1984, and he announced its organization April 2, 1985—eleven months before the March was to set off. To bring his dream into being, he had assembled a staff which grew to include 150 men and women, mostly quite young and mostly white. They had been drawn by Mixner's vision and charisma, but, according to Howard Cushner, PRO-Peace director of communications, writing in *Mother Jones*, "few were prepared to recognize or deal with what

16

came to be PRO-Peace's biggest problem: David Mixner operated as if he were accountable to no one."

This staff, highly centralized and with the help of numerous volunteers, set about raising funds and recruiting Marchers, each of whom was supposed to raise and turn over to PRO-Peace $3,200—a dollar for each mile in the March from Los Angeles to Washington.

The big corporate donations that Mixner had confidently predicted did not materialize, but big bills did flow in. Instead of the 5,000 Marchers hoped for, only 1,200 had signed up and been accepted by PRO-Peace in the last days of February, and these 1,200 brought with them an average of only $700 each. The March was paralyzed before it took its first steps from the assembly point in White Oak National Guard Armory in Los Angeles onto the sizzling streets of the city—the temperature was 94 degrees. And already Mixner had begun to suggest that the faint of heart had better go home.

By no means were all those people who had given up their homes, their jobs, their whole way of life ready to meekly admit defeat before they had even gotten started on their effort to conquer the continent—on their effort to make a real contribution to nuclear disarmament. Consider, for example, this handful of people who were ready to start walking toward the opposite coast:

Shirley Carter, a 38-year-old Black woman was born with cerebral palsy. Although doctors prophesied she could never walk, she decided as a young child that she would prove them wrong. Not only did she learn to walk, she became a social worker. Now that her son was successfully into his last year in high school, she would not lightly drop out of a March she thought was very important.

Shirley Carter.

Neither would Dale Malleck, a retired metalworker from Denver. At age 57 Dale had had open-heart surgery and to recover his health he started walking. He also began using his retirement years to go to college, which had never been possible before, because he had a retarded son to support. The opportunity to be in a movement of real service to humanity, which the March represented to Dale, was not something he would easily abandon.

Shinohora Kazue, a 21-year-old student activist had come all the way from Japan to express her belief that "the nuclear buildup is

When I tell people that I completed the entire distance in eight-and-a-half months, I can only hope that they look at me as an average person who decided to do something for peace, and the question in their minds has to be, "Why not me?"

–Madonna Newburg, Marcher

wrong," and she was not about to take the next plane back to her homeland. "When I see something that is wrong, I have to do something about it," she said to people who wanted to know her story.

Madonna Newburg, 57, a retired school teacher, had worked long and hard in the Catholic Workers movement and in the nuclear freeze movement. To her the idea of giving up the March with its high objectives was simply unthinkable.

Daniel Chavez, 34, a Chicano, was the sole PRO-Peace attorney who would not abandon the March. The child of migrant farm workers, he remembered the stories his grandmother had told about the hardships she faced as she walked with her children all the way from south of Mexico City to Los Angeles. Dan could not be a party to efforts to demobilize the March.

Nor could Mauricio Terrazas, 69, a truck driver, long active in a rank and file movement opposing the gangster-ridden leadership of the Teamsters Union.

Those who came with their children and who formed the group later known as Family Town, were not going home, either. They connected deeply with one another and decided they would cross the United States for peace no matter what the rest of the Marchers did.

These people and others like them were on hand when the dazzling rock concert send-off that had been planned turned out to be a much scaled-down affair. Six thousand supporters at City Hall, not 100,000 at the Coliseum, said their farewells to the 1,200—not the predicted 5,000—Marchers as they started eastward.

Crowds along the streets were abundant only in East Los Angeles where there was warm support from the huge Hispanic community. Marcher Elizabeth Radcliffe, 22, of Oakland, California, recalls meeting the eyes of a woman standing at the curb that day. The woman was crying. Elizabeth reached out and took her hands. "You're walking for me, too," the woman said.

A March supporter, Edith Sullwold, who walked with us the first day, was struck by the gratitude of people in the ethnic communities. "Mothers holding children, families, old people, some crying, mostly smiling and waving and wishing the Marchers good luck—the words I heard most from them were, 'Thanks a lot.' That sense of gratitude to the Marchers for making a statement for peace and for life was for me very profound."

However, that show of support was not enough to buoy up some of the less resolute Marchers. Certain amenities that PRO-Peace had promised were lacking. More than a few urban middleclass individuals who had responded to the slick PRO-Peace propaganda found they couldn't do without the mobile showers and laundry they had been promised. Numbers began to dwindle.

Lack of money caused problems of other kinds. Not only the legal staff, with the exception of Dan Chavez, but also the medical staff of PRO-Peace had resigned. Neither they nor other staff members had been paid for weeks. Moreover, the March could not pay for liability insurance which was being demanded at each place where a PRO-Peace advance team had sought a campsite. On the third day, March 3, the city officials of Claremont revoked permission they had granted for the use of a site.

Here the first of many astonishing rescues kept the March alive. The reservoir of peace sentiment that existed in churches and the Claremont Colleges became apparent, and by a prodigy of organization, local residents provided beds, showers and meals for the main body of Marchers.

Gaynl Trotter, wife of a professor in the School of Theology, Claremont Graduate School, was the volunteer chairperson of the Claremont welcoming committee. She recalls, "We found out on Friday afternoon that the March wasn't going to get insurance and on Saturday morning I alerted the churches." The church organizations quickly found homes for most of the Marchers for the night and provided space on church grounds for the others and their tents. Months later Gaynl looked back: "The March was one of the most exciting things that has happened to Claremont. It was a unifying thing that brought all kinds of people together. The religious community came through."

Torie Osborn, PRO-Peace staffer, later remembered, "We learned [from Claremont] there is need to interact with the community. The lesson came because of site insurance. Not having that insurance may have been the best thing that could have happened to us."

When I think of what I used to care about, like washing my hair daily and blow-drying it, I can only shake my head.

—Marcher

Claremont was a mini-miracle that we would remember and talk about for the next eight and one-half months. It also provided the prototype for a Marcher-in-the-Home (MITH) program that continued across the country and became one of our most successful forms of outreach.

Robert Blake, star of the TV shows *Baretta* and *HellTown*, attached himself to the March in its initial days. With his sense of the theatrical he was an effective fund-raiser. At Claremont he got a good many dollars transferred from pockets to trash bags he had passed around among the people who came to greet the Marchers.

After leaving Claremont, we headed for Chaffey College along a road that was often uphill under a sky that was always hot. Encouragement was welcome and it came at one point from construction workers who had nailed up a sign: NO NUKES. Encouragement came again when children poured out of an elementary school, carrying the musical instruments they were learning to play. At the edge of the road, the kids stretched out their hands to touch ours and we walked single file so we could touch theirs. A group of little ones cheered, did cartwheels and somersaults and chorused out, "Yea, Peace!"

Gestures of support appeared in many forms. While we were camped in Glen Helen Park in San Bernardino County, a nearby nudist camp offered free bathing facilities—an offer that was gladly accepted by some weary people, including whole families, who had been inside their warm clothing on a very hot day.

Like the Claremont city fathers, officials of San Bernardino County were not bent on making life easy for the March. They threatened—and carried out—close inspections of kitchen facilities. Highway officials announced restrictions that forced all Marchers except a token few off Cajon Pass, which connects the Los Angeles basin and the Mojave Desert. Because a frontage road was lacking there, the March as a whole had to undergo the indignity of being expensively bussed a few miles.

Rain added to our woes—cold rain. By the end of the tenth day—at the edge of the Mojave Desert—twelve Marchers had hypothermia, a dangerous drop in body temperature. "It was raining and by mile twelve the mud was ankle deep," recalls Marcher Hugh Burleton. "At first the rain felt warm, but then the temperature dropped, down into the thirties, I suppose...The wind was blowing

We found the Marchers in Hesperia [CA] in this awful sandstorm, and here are all these people laughing and smiling and happy. I thought they were crazy.

—Jean Parker,
Apple Valley, CA,
who later joined the March

20

Walking into a storm in the Mojave desert

40 or 50 miles an hour." Hugh continues, "A few of us ended up wandering around in a kind of stupor. I couldn't find my tent and I didn't know what to do. I think some of us would have died, but some of our fellow Marchers got us dried off, put us in warm clothes and fed us soup."

Hypothermia had been diagnosed by medical doctors among the Marchers, all but two of whom would soon leave. However, help in another form soon came from the medical world: Physicians for Social Responsibility sent a check for $7,500.

At a campground on Bureau of Land Management property on Stoddard Wells Road, ten miles west of Barstow, the March settled down in the mud on the afternoon of March 10.

We joined hands in solidarity when we were abandoned at Stoddard Wells Road in the Mojave Desert.

*Since 1981
preparations for
war have cost each
American family
$21,000.*
  *–Center for Defense
  Information, 1987*

With the aid of remaining PRO-Peace staff members, four of whom served on an initial Policy Board, Marchers began to set up their own primitive and vaguely defined form of self-government. Soon they forced the resignation of the four PRO-Peace staff members and set about holding elections.

Elections started at the bottom. Each pair of Marchers had been assigned a top-of-the-line North Face tent that was either blue, yellow, orange or red. The blue tents were supposed to be set up around a big blue tent called a town hall. The red tents were to cluster around a red town hall, and so on. Each of these clusters was a "town" and in each town were several tents that constituted a "village" (both the "town" and "village" distinctions later tended to disappear).

Each town now held a town meeting attended by Marchers assigned to it. A few days before, most of us had been total strangers to each other and now we were being asked to choose community leaders. The technique we worked out was this: at each town meeting, anyone willing to serve on a central governing body stood up and made known his or her qualifications. Many described their volunteer experience as organizers in one or another peace group. Some had held government jobs or had been involved in social work. Franklin told of research he had done on the history of the armies of unemployed that had crossed the continent in 1894, in 1931 and 1932. Even with the help of these self-nominated candidates, it was difficult to know how to select little-known persons for tasks that were even less well-known—in fact, were almost totally undefined.

But from each of the four town meetings emerged a representative to a Policy Board, who was empowered to vote, and an alternate, who could speak but not vote.* These representatives began to try to deal with the problem that was now clear—the imminent collapse of PRO-Peace.

On March 14, Board members were in session in one of the big town hall tents when—unknown to them—a helicopter touched down in the camp. David Mixner stepped out of the chopper, briefly announced to those who gathered around him that PRO-Peace no

---

* Members of the Policy Board were: Thomas Atlee, Steven Carillo, Trevor Darvill, Franklin Folsom, Judith Rane, Jerry Rubin, Robert Trausch and either Mary Giardina or Dona Ridgeway (they rotated).

longer existed and apologized for "personal inconvenience" to their lives. Then he left. We were on our own. The leaders of our fledgling self-government, the Policy Board, did not find out until after the helicopter flew off that Mixner had been in camp.

The failure of Mixner's dream had been anticipated months before by staff members in Los Angeles. Tim Carpenter and Allan Affeldt of the Field department had been particularly outspoken about the need to scale down the March to a more realistic 1,000 Marchers and a staff of two dozen. Mixner and his supporters met this with hostility and said, "If you don't believe in it, you will be the one who makes it fail."

In November Dan Chavez, the attorney, had joined Tim and Allan in the Field department. By February it was clear to the three of them that PRO-Peace was doomed, and they met with a sympathetic businessman to ask him what he thought the options were. He said two possibilities existed which would enable the March to continue: one was bankruptcy, in which case Mixner would resign and release control to a trustee; the other possibility was to form a new corporation. The bankruptcy option was suggested to Mixner, but he dismissed the idea.

Two days earlier, on March 12, Coleen Ashly, who worked for PRO-Peace in transportation, was told by her immediate supervisor that PRO-Peace was about to fold and that she was to collect the keys to all the vehicles, then wake the drivers in the middle of the night so they could return everything to Los Angeles. According to rumors, it was Mixner's idea that when the Marchers woke up the next morning they would find themselves in the middle of the desert with none of the vehicles essential for survival. What would they do without porta-potties or a kitchen, a refrigerator truck or trailers? Their only option would be to go home.

Coleen did collect all the keys, but instead of keeping them, she set up a system of rotating them among four trusted individuals. When Robert the "repo-man" finally appeared, there were no keys to be found.

"The next night [March 13] my boss came with an attorney and a thug," Coleen remembers. "They were going to dump everything out in the desert and take all the vehicles." They had arranged for three U-Haul tractors and drivers to pick up the trailers on Saturday,

The dream is not dead. Others have taken over the skeleton of PRO-Peace...and vowed to...make it across the continent in a walking lobby for nuclear disarmament.

–Marc Cooper,
L.A. Weekly,
March 21, 1986

but Coleen persuaded the U-Haul owner to wait until Monday to carry out the plan. The extra two days would give us time to walk to the town of Barstow, where reorganization could begin.

Later that day, a similar plan was agreed to by the owner of the refrigerator truck. Dan Chavez met with Coleen on Saturday to assure her she was not going to prison and that she should release the vehicles only to people who had court orders to take possession of them. The earliest date on which PRO-Peace could get such orders would be Monday, March 17, so we had a little time in which to maneuver. Frantic negotiations over a phone ten miles from camp saved the kitchen, at least temporarily. Dan Chavez and a Los Angeles supporter, Fred Segal, worked out a plan to pay the present and past due bills for the kitchen, so that we could hold onto it until Las Vegas. Without coordination or much knowledge about what others in camp were doing, individual Marchers began to make phone calls to potential rescuers.

Meg Gage, executive director of the Peace Development Fund, in Amherst, Massachusetts, found herself on the receiving end of many calls. "I finally latched onto the porta-potty thing," she said. "The toilets were something I could raise money for." And she did.

Help from supporters depended on a communication link between the marooned March and the outside world. The media had buried us. How could word get out that the GPM was alive but in need of aid?

Richard Polese, a Marcher who had known and written about Peace Pilgrim,* heard that a minister in Barstow had offered to help. Richard hitched a ride to town and called Rev. Glenn Schultz of the First Congregational Church. He said he'd been waiting for us and asked what he could provide. "I told him we needed the use of a phone for a few days, and he said we could use the church's office phone," Richard says. "I remember telling him we might interrupt the routine there for a couple of days. What an understatement that turned out to be!"

If we stand silent in the face of an arms race...we must share responsibility for the outcome. "Silence gives consent."
—*Bruce Russett,*
The Prisoners of Insecurity

---

* Peace Pilgrim was a woman who in 1953 began a pilgrimage across the United States that was to last 28 years. She walked alone, with no outside support and accepting no money; she declared *"I shall walk until given shelter and fast until given food. I shall remain a wanderer until mankind has learned the ways of peace."* Charismatic in a simple way, using her life as an example, she has become almost a saint to many in the peace movement. Peace Pilgrim died in 1981.

Richard immediately rang the PRO-Peace answering service and told the operator to reroute calls for the March to the new Barstow number. Within a few seconds the first call came in and the phone didn't stop ringing for the next three or four days. Richard heard from concerned parents, from GPM people in regional offices around the country, from media reporters—and from PRO-Peace creditors. Fortunately, he had taken his sleeping bag and some other gear when he left Stoddard Wells. "I camped right there in the office catching a few winks between rings," he says. "Over the hours, the structure, support and supply systems and logistics of the reborn March began to come together."

Marcher Diane Hara dashed off to Los Angeles to coordinate an office of volunteers which became the new home office in Santa Monica. Working with non-Marcher volunteer Joyce Staton, they got some of the first relief supplies and equipment together.

Even before Mixner's announcement, people began to gather in groups to explore alternative plans for continuing the March without PRO-Peace. Clearly, some of us were not going to give up. From one meeting two possibilities emerged: to hang together and proceed with as many people as possible or to break up into small self-contained groups. These alternatives became known as Plan A and Plan B.

As discussion of the plans went on, and even before the election of the Policy Board, task forces developed. These grew out of a blueprint for organization that PRO-Peace had designed: each Marcher was to do volunteer work to keep the March functioning. Accordingly, people now signed up for duty preparing vegetables in the kitchen, washing dishes, getting water tanks filled, cleaning the porta-potties. And so on. Each group of people who worked together evolved into a functioning unit—a task force—and from these task forces more than 30 departments eventually developed.

A group of volunteers that formed to collect and recycle litter had begun functioning before the GPM even left Los Angeles. Diane Clark, an elementary school teacher who later became Peace City's ceremonial mayor, began to organize litter pickup in Griffith Park, the Los Angeles campsite just before departure. "Litter-consciousness was established from the first day," according to Diane.

So it went through the most basic phases of existence of this developing community from which much of the centralized structure supplied by PRO-Peace staff members was disappearing. Some functions were still being performed by former PRO-Peace staff—now volunteers—but many Marchers tended to attribute Mixner's mistakes to all who had worked for him. It was a case of guilt by association. As a result many of the former staff members left the March feeling isolated and rejected, as indeed they were. Yet some stayed and provided leadership and at least ten completed the March to Washington.

Meeting for hours in a town hall tent at Stoddard Wells, the Policy Board tried to check up on and correlate the functions of the different task forces. At the same time, volunteers went to the town of Barstow and searched for a better site—one nearer to phones, to stores and to people who might help. The local community college declined to let us use its facilities, ostensibly because we did not have liability insurance, but some Marchers thought there were other more political reasons. No other site appeared feasible.

And then Linzy Franklin, manager of the BMX bicycle race track, was moved by the plight of the abandoned but still hopeful community at Stoddard Wells. He had space near the track and he invited us to set up camp there. In hope and some excitement we took down our tents and walked the ten miles to Barstow.

Now the distance to phones and the main street of town was less than half a mile. On BMX property, next to a junkyard, serious reorganization began. The March had now been on the road 16 days.

On March 19, at the request of the Policy Board, Allan Affeldt, Dan Chavez and a third Marcher, Diane Shea, who happened to be available in Los Angeles, incorporated the Great Peace March for Global Nuclear Disarmament. (The word "global" was inserted to let the public know that Marchers wanted all countries to "take down the bomb.") Now, under California law, Affeldt, Chavez and Shea had full power to run the affairs of the March, but when they accepted the proposal that they act as incorporators, they had promised that they would resign from their posts if the Marchers at any time wished a different set of officers—a situation that did arise before long.

The experience of Affeldt and Chavez was invaluable in the initial stages of fund-raising, as was the energizing participation of

Tim Carpenter, former field director of PRO-Peace. Within twenty-four hours after Mixner announced the collapse of his organization, those three had managed to assemble $15,000 in cash, checks and pledges; all this even before they filed for incorporation as a non-profit, educational organization that hoped to receive (and later did receive) tax-exempt status. On March 17—still before incorporation—Carpenter announced that several Great Peace March volunteer offices had opened up across the country along the route that the March was expected to follow. These were all offices staffed by persons who had been working for PRO-Peace and then had switched to volunteer status.

In camp, Tom Atlee set about coordinating further fundraising activities by Marchers themselves. Phone calls went out all over the country to family members and friends and others who had contributed toward the entrance fees of Marchers. It was not easy to tell these contributors that most of the money they had given had vanished into some kind of black hole, that more was needed to continue the important work of trying to rouse large numbers of people to speak out against nuclear weapons. But contributions began to arrive, some from sources that had not been forthcoming as long as PRO-Peace ran the show. The driver of a truck carrying a load of PRO-Peace T-shirts parked at the camp entrance and began to sell T-shirts to curious sightseers. Did the shirts—and the profits from their sale—belong to the March? This was not clear, but money contributed at a table set up near the campground entrance did belong to the March. To it local citizens brought cash. A woman drove out from Los Angeles with $500 and left it—but not her name—at the contribution table. One supporter appeared with a truckload of strawberries. Another, from Arizona, drove into camp with several hundred pounds of honey.

The Barstow Church of God in Christ, a Black congregation, and its related parochial school provided meeting space, a lavish lunch and a concert of gospel music for us one day. In the middle of the concert the drums played by a talented 12-year-old boy broke. A hat was passed among the Marchers so that the school could buy a new set. Zadie Dunmore, the school secretary, said a year later, "The children remember where the drums came from and they enjoy playing them. That was great." The church pastor, Bishop Nathaniel Jones, told of the impact the Marchers had on the children: they started looking for articles about the GPM, and the March became the subject for essays and poems. "The March became part of the

While we were marching on March 21: Chinese premier Zho Ziyang announces reduced military budget and an end to aboveground nuclear tests.

27

*Dear Friends,
I thank you for
going through the
Peace March. It
takes a real
generous person to
do what you are
doing. I will help
as much as I can
by keeping some
peace. I hope you
make it. Go for it!*

*–Todd Stump,
Grade 5,
Skyline North Central
School, Barstow, CA*

28

children's daily prayers," said Bishop Jones. "It definitely raised their consciousness about the arms race."

As an expression of gratitude for what the Church of God in Christ had done for us, Marcher Sadnah Lembo designed a huge thank you card which all available Marchers signed. This was given to Bishop Jones. A similar card went to Linzy Franklin of the BMX Track. Both still had the cards a year later and displayed them very proudly.

A beauty parlor in Barstow gave us free haircuts. A motel owner, a native of India, impressed by the Gandhi-like attitude of some of the Marchers, contributed showers. Workers in the shops of the Santa Fe Railway collected money among themselves to buy hundreds of pairs of socks for Marchers. The nascent Policy Board had not thought of asking for socks, but it did put together a wish list which the new Media department tried to get widely circulated. Soon a lot of people knew some of the things the stranded March needed: a refrigerator truck; a dry food storage trailer; two 2,500-plus gallon water haulers; two diesel generators; diesel, gasoline and propane fuel; 12-volt deep cycle batteries; large meeting tents or yurts; communication equipment; a medical support vehicle; regular supplies of nutritious food; battery-powered camping lanterns; cash in any amount; a ten-ton capacity floor jack; several large truck trailers and a tractor; a computer and printer; the services of licensed doctors.

Day after day organizing and planning continued and Alden Sievers of the Bureau of Land Management (BLM) looked on. It was he who would have to decide whether or not to let us walk and camp in the desert for ten days. He did not consider vetoing the March because of its objective, but he frankly wondered if the Marchers knew enough about roughing it to get through the desert without suffering serious casualties. If they couldn't handle themselves, he didn't want to be responsible for giving out permits that might lead to disaster.

The more Sievers saw, the more he became convinced that the estimated 350 Marchers who remained in Barstow were serious, responsible citizens. At the Stoddard Wells Road BLM site they had left the campsite perfectly clean. They used their spare time in Barstow picking up trash along the city streets—three hundred bags full. They listened when he talked of practical problems—such as open, unmarked mine shafts near the remote dirt powerline road Marchers would have to follow and cautions about the Mojave's rattlesnakes. Also, there were turns in the narrow dirt road around which larger vehicles could not go. A stalled vehicle at one of these turns could hold up the entire March, far from help.

After Sievers brought up these problems, teams of Marchers went out to see for themselves the conditions they would have to face. When they returned and Sievers became convinced that the March would acquit itself well, he issued the necessary permits. Later he wrote a letter praising our conservation policies and good citizenship. This letter opened up many campsites along the way that might otherwise have been closed.

Meantime, on the BMX campground, Marchers moved about like amoebas seen in a drop of water under a microscope. They coalesced into groups that sometimes grew larger, sometimes split up into smaller groups. And in all of them there was talk, planning, theorizing about what should be done to save the March. As these spontaneous meetings went on, so too did the work of the departments that were developing to keep Peace City functioning.

It soon became clear that the Policy Board could not adequately oversee the work of these departments, a dozen or more of which would be needed as the community resumed its daily moves across the country. Created—or re-created—at Barstow were groups dealing with campscape (the design of and care for each campsite), sanitation, transportation, mail, water, kitchen, security, medical matters, information-communication, media (public information)— and childcare and schools.

Clearly there had to be some individual who would devote full time to studying the problems in each department and helping the departments coordinate their work—a kind of city manager. At the same time there were strong tendencies, expressed by a sizeable number of Marchers, against any centralized authority. They had been burned by PRO-Peace, which had been highly centralized, and they sought some form of organization over which Marchers could exert democratic or consensual control.

Finally, an Operations Council developed, with representatives from each functioning department of the community, and for a while one person met with this council and all its separate divisions and

I wondered why somebody didn't do something for peace, then I remembered that I am somebody.

–Marcher

acted as liaison between the operational departments. Later, the burdens of this often thankless job were divided up among three persons who became known as City Managers. Each one had a few special departments with which he or she kept in touch.

As all this organizing and planning went forward at Barstow, accompanied by endless meetings, Marchers grew restless. Some could not bear to wait and a few small groups implemented plan B and took off on their own. The largest of these, a contingent of thirteen calling themselves the Peace Wave, conducted their own march on a route more or less paralleling the general route outlined by PRO-Peace and which the Great Peace March finally followed. The Peace Wave people crossed paths with the GPM in the major cities and met the main body of Marchers again on the East Coast. Along the way the thirteen used GPM tents and were no doubt aided in their solicitation of food and funds by the publicity generated by the central body of the March. They supported themselves independently but did not contribute to solving any of the knotty organizational problems with which the GPM had to deal. Yet they did reach many communities which otherwise might not have heard about or had contact with other Marchers, and they were always welcomed warmly when they intersected with the GPM.

Another potential split became more serious at Barstow. Shanawa, a Mescalero Apache, who had been sent into the March with funds provided by other Native Americans, campaigned strenuously for a change of route so that the March could go by Big Mountain in Arizona. There, a major confrontation was about to take place between a group of Navajos and their supporters and United States marshals who were scheduled to evict them from lands on which they had lived for a very long time. Marchers were sympathetic to the plight of the Native Americans, but questioned the wisdom of such a distraction from their major objective—nuclear disarmament—to help the Hopi and Navajo people. No doubt, all along the way across the country there would be worthy causes in which Marchers would want to participate, but could the March hold together, if it allowed itself to digress each time a worthy cause appeared on the horizon?

This issue was not quickly settled. Urged by Shanawa and Big Mountain activists who set up a table in the middle of camp, some Marchers went off to Big Mountain. The Policy Board voted to send an official delegation to investigate what connection there might be between the Big Mountain controversy and the cause of nuclear disarmament. One was claimed: according to the Big Mountain Legal Defense and Offense Committee, commercial mining interests supposedly wanted access to coal and uranium deposits that could be mined in the Big Mountain area. And uranium is necessary for the production of nuclear weapons.

After hearing a report from the delegation to Big Mountain, the Policy Board sent a letter of support to the Native Americans who were trying to keep possession of their land. But the Policy Board declined to divert the whole March to the long route that led through the Big Mountain area. For one thing, time was pressing, if the March was to reach Washington before winter. Also there was a possible rendezvous on July 30, at Davenport, Iowa, with the Mississippi Peace Cruise in which a Soviet delegation was taking part with American citizens. If the March could make up time lost at Barstow, it could make a big gesture of international friendship at Davenport.

Not only Big Mountain seized our attention. Native Americans appeared in camp and invited Marchers to join in their sunrise ceremonies. People with other religious interests began to seek each other out. Some Marchers took up the practice of forming circles and holding hands, sometimes in silence, sometimes while speaking out whatever was on their minds. This custom then spilled over into the Policy Board and soon-to-be established City Council—a kind of intrusion of Church into State.*

On and on the meetings went. At the same time, more vehicles appeared in camp. Souter Ford Agency in Barstow contributed an old school bus. Marchers Bob Alei and Bill Van Matre bought another school bus and lent it to the March. Luckily, there were skilled mechanics in camp. They disemboweled the vehicles and put them in running order. (For more detail about the mechanics see Chapter IV.) A dentist, Mordecai Roth, had given money to PRO-Peace for a downpayment on a motor home, in which he installed a dental chair and other professional equipment. After the bankruptcy he repurchased the vehicle so that it stayed with the March. (PRO-Peace had kept the downpayment.) Roger McAfee, a farmer, came

Navajo Indians who went down into the uranium mines have died–and are right now dying–of lung cancer, previously rare among Navajos.
–Ken Keyes
The Hundreth Monkey

---

* By-law: Each scheduled City Council meeting will use the folowing form: Opening Rite. The Council members will take a moment to reaffirm their commitment to a cooperative process at the beginning of each meeting. This moment should also include a time for silence to reflect on our common commitment to global nuclear disarmamnent.

in one night and on behalf of his organization contributed a haybaler. At first glance a haybaler seemed about the last thing the March needed, but it was self-propelled. The driver sat out ahead of the front wheels, and it could carry an amazing amount of the equipment that a mobile community would need. "The haybaler was like a ridiculous erector set," says Brian Goldman, who drove it into Chicago at 4 a.m. five months later. "You couldn't shift it, and it had no brakes." But it held up until South Bend, Indiana, where it died a quiet death.

Another farmer appeared with offers of tractors and other vehicles if the March would give him unquestioned control of the whole venture. After their experience with centralized control under Mixner, Marchers were wary of giving total authority to anybody. The farmer's offer was not accepted, although it was loudly debated with the aid of a bullhorn in the center of camp.

But what was the alternative? Everyone had his or her own idea. Katea Golub, who had had experience in organizing with the 1984 Olympic Games, prepared an organizational chart, displayed it in the center of camp and lectured on the merits of a strong organization with authority delegated to assistants. Other organization charts began to surface.

During their stay in Barstow, many Marchers were not content to idle away time in the hospitable town which provided them shelter, showers and food. Those not engaged in the reorganization process spent hours saying thanks to Barstow. Some cleaned trash from the city parks and from the roads leading into town, others gave a fresh coat of paint to the community center; some made repairs on the Mojave River Valley Museum and a volunteer workforce was set up to do odd jobs for local homeowners.

But what was most needed to hold the restless throng together was movement toward its announced goal. And on the morning of March 28, movement began. Residents of Barstow can still see the farewell message painted on the junkyard fence next to the bicycle track. Huge red and blue letters read: THE PEACE MARCHERS THANK YOU.

The March headed out of Barstow on a service road under a high-voltage power line that ran toward Las Vegas. Las Vegas, everyone hoped, would provide money and public awareness that

The Soviets are not the enemy, they are the excuse for making money.

–Dr. Helen Caldicott

As we hiked out of Barstow March 28 we left a sign THE PEACE MARCHERS THANK YOU.

the March was alive and moving. Already almost a hundred ambassadors, some self-appointed, had gone out ahead to arrange for fund-raising there. Another 150 or so had gone to their homes or to other places to get personal vehicles or funds to be used by the March. The total number of those who considered themselves part of the ongoing effort may have been about 600 at this time.

Chapter II

Order Out Of Chaos

March 28 : Yermo, CA
April 4-7 : Near Whiskey Pete's, NV
April 12 : Las Vegas, NV
April 22-23 : St.George, UT
May 8-9 : Grand Junction, CO
May 18-19 : Vail, CO
May 29-31 : Denver, CO

Peace City had taken a major step toward self-government on March 27. That day about 95 percent of the Marchers voted in favor of having a City Council that would replace the Policy Board. Then they proceded to elect eight members of the Council itself.*

Consensus would be the preferred method the Council used in reaching decisions—not the more familiar, quicker practice of

---

* The first City Council members were: Thomas Atlee, Steven Carillo, Evan Conroy, Franklin Folsom, Judith McConnell, Judith Rane and any two of these representing Family Town: Lindy Flynn, Dona Ridgeway or Robert Trausch.

carrying on business by majority vote. There was to be no imposition of the will of a majority on a minority, if that could be avoided. But a provision in the by-laws of the new governing body did allow a vote if a decision could not be reached otherwise. A facilitator, who was not a member of the Council, would preside over the meetings.

The governing apparatus of the March now consisted of two complementary, and sometimes contradictory, elements—a City Council that derived such authority as it had from the Marchers, and a Board of Directors that was a formal legal entity, recognized by the State of California where the GPM was incorporated.

In the coming days, the outgoing Policy Board members began a process of familiarizing the incoming Council members with their duties. The Board members sat near Council members on the floor of a town hall tent and gave information to their replacements when such help seemed to be needed. And the Council members did indeed need help, outside the Council meetings as well as in them. Anywhere, at any time in camp, Marchers came up to them with suggestions, complaints and questions, questions, questions. More than one Council member envied Marcher Bill Van Matre who wore a cap that bore this legend in large letters: I DON'T KNOW.

We were 500 shepherds in search of a flock.

—*Marcher*

No Moses had appeared who could lead the exodus of Marchers from Barstow, nor did the vast majority of Marchers seek one. But a committee—the City Council—was a kind of central leadership.

With a United States flag, a homemade "world unity flag" and a Great Peace March banner at the head of the line, 350 Marchers strode out of Barstow at 6:45 a.m., March 28. Because of repeated warnings about poisonous snakes, three self-appointed monitors formed a "critter analysis" patrol. One walked ahead in the narrow road. The other two walked in the scraggly vegetation on either side of the road. Their aim was to warn Marchers if snakes were about, although some observed it was more of an exercise in machismo than a real safeguard. Even with this precaution a rattlesnake did go unnoticed under a shrub at the side of the road, and for the first time in their lives a number of Marchers heard the frightening dry sound a rattler makes when it is coiled, ready to strike.

Because of our mission, we wanted to be visible and noticed by fellow citizens, but California highway officials would not allow us to walk along the shoulder of Interstate 15 between Barstow and Las Vegas. This heavily traveled thoroughfare was too dangerous, they said, for use by pedestrians, and there was no continuous frontage road along this stretch that would permit safe pedestrian passage. Too many gamblers dashed along the interstate at high speed to get from Los Angeles to the gaming tables in Nevada. Too many drunks drove back along it from Las Vegas to Los Angeles. The Marchers had no choice but to spend ten days in the desert where only the coyotes and lizards would see the flag that identified the Great Peace March for Global Nuclear Disarmament.

In the desert, the City Council began the task of trying to find exactly how many people planned to take the hike to Washington—that is, how many mouths there were to feed. To help in this process, photo ID cards were issued to all who agreed to abide by whatever rules and regulations came into being for the community as a whole. Dan Chavez, the lawyer among the three original officers in the corporation, drafted a simple agreement or contract, not unlike the one PRO-Peace had required of all March applicants. This document required anyone who signed it to forego the use of alcohol or drugs in camp, to have a medical exam, to behave peacefully and to obey such rules as might become necessary.

Easter Sunday afternoon Dan arrived in camp with copies of this agreement and began to ask for signatures. The day that had begun with a tape recording of Handel's *Messiah* as a wakeup call, now turned into a noisy rebellion. This was in jarring contrast to the joyous Easter egg hunt which the children had prepared. All morning they had colored eggs—one for each Marcher—and hidden them at the afternoon campsite. The hunt was quickly forgotten when it became clear that a number of Marchers would have nothing to do with an agreement they had not helped to draft—nothing to do with a contract proposed by a former PRO-Peace staff member—and Dan fell into this category. The camp seemed split right down the middle on the issue of whether to sign or not to sign the form Dan considered essential to the March's progress.

In an open space in the center of Peace City Marchers milled around and some shouted angrily. No meeting had been called. No one was in charge. Several speakers tried to create order, but chaos was the only result.

The Great Peace March is a study in organized confusion.

–Warren Strobel,
Washington Times

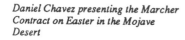

Daniel Chavez presenting the Marcher Contract on Easter in the Mojave Desert

The rebellion of a vocal segment against the contract was intense, although many other Marchers were perfectly willing to sign. Chavez had one-on-one conferences with Marchers who pleaded reasons of conscience for refusing to sign and made a series of compromise drafts of the contract. In the end he gave up. Those who refused to sign any form of the new contract continued on the March, making it clear that the City Council and the Board of Directors could not enforce certain critical decisions. At the same time, the rebels made it difficult to determine how many committed Marchers there were, as distinct from freeloaders who began to attach themselves to the March in Barstow.

In support of the IDs, Dan said, "We Marchers know of other Marchers in this camp who have harmed our March image with vandalism, thefts and indifference to order. Yet I sense a great deal of patience with these individuals, not equally extended to the Board of Directors."

The tension remained from this day on between those who believed the March would be most effective if there were a central structure and organization and those who felt comfortable only if citywide consensus were used for all decisions. Some of the people who felt it too restrictive to sign a Marcher agreement later coalesced into a group who became known as the Anarchists and who, as a group, would put up their tents around a black flag.

The volunteer security officers were helpless to screen who was and who wasn't a bonafide Marcher. Some of them had little experience or training in getting compliance with rules and none had come on the March to be a cop. It was not easy in a community that constantly emphasized its commitment to nonviolence to build up a law enforcement apparatus, and there was a pervasive attitude that we should not call in the local police.

Frequently, chaos in the security department spilled over into other phases of community life. For example, what could be done about individuals who wanted to tag along with the March, although they seemingly had little to contribute to it? Some of these had come aboard when PRO-Peace, in a frantic attempt to fill out the ranks, had accepted people who, for one reason or another, were really unfit to walk across the country in the name of peace. Others had simply walked into camp and stayed.

An unofficial entrance-exit committee had established itself at Barstow to screen prospective Marchers. But how could people be added without repeating the mistakes of PRO-Peace? The entrance-exit committee required applicants to fill out a questionnaire, to appear before the committee for an interview and have a physical exam to make sure they would not bring any communicable diseases into camp or collapse under the rigors of the March.

In the early days of the GPM when there was barely enough money to meet the needs of the regular Marchers, 20 or so new people had turned up. Most of them were making important contributions, but some were not. Before we reached Las Vegas, the entrance-exit committee began the process of screening new people to determine who among them could serve the March well and to ask those who were causing problems to leave. In the latter category a man who called himself "Jesus" insisted that the March provide him and several of his followers with food and shelter. He could prove his identity, too. JESUS was tattooed on his thigh. When he realized he was not going to be admitted to Peace City, he appeared at a City Council meeting, loomed over the Council members sitting on the ground and intoned, "I disempower you," and left. But he was not gone long. Two days later he rode past the March on a new bicycle, possibly financed by funds he had been seen soliciting in the name of the GPM.

The Great Peace March is now totally democratic. It's run by the people. Everything is done by consensus. It may take us six days to decide where to park the porta-potties, but everything is a group decision.

–Lee Bush, Marcher

March 23, 1986: The third anniversary of President Reagan's speech proposing his SDI or Star Wars program.

At another point, a man appeared and handed out his business card with his worldly name on one side and CHRIST II on the other. When not busy being Christ, he made his living, so he said, as a blackjack player. He worked in camp and might have stayed for a while, but he was found offering candy to little girls to entice them into his tent. When discovered, he had to be decisively separated from the March. The Judicial Board, which had been set up to handle conflicts, possible infractions of Peace City rules and other community problems, did not have the authority to physically remove anyone who was unwilling to go. The Peace City security force was not equal to the task, so the local police had to be called in. For a community of its size, Peace City had remarkably few incidents of violence, but violence was a form of behavior for which a few individuals were removed from the March.

Another unresolved governmental problem was the relationship between the City Council and the three-member Board of Directors which had exclusive legal power to run the March. Marchers who mistrusted the Board, because it was made up of former PRO-Peace employees, now called on the Board members to honor the promise to resign which they had given when they were asked to incorporate the March. In their place a March-elected board would take over. Allan Affeldt was reluctant to resign, but he finally agreed to a compromise: the three original incorporators would remain on the Board alongside four new members to be elected by the Marchers.

Another in a steady stream of elections took place before the GPM reached Nevada, and four new members were added to the Board.* The democratic process had produced a body on which elected members could be a majority, if they so chose. From that point on, the Board of Directors would be in charge of general March policy and what might be called foreign affairs— relations with the outside world—but internal matters and daily March decisions were the City Council's responsibility.

Meetings of the City Council, of the new Board of Directors, of a variety of special interest groups (gays, lesbians, committees with plans to publish leaflets, manifestos, news bulletins,** teachers, seniors, religious groups) filled the late afternoons and evenings

---

* The new Board members were Coleen Ashly, Evan Conroy, Franklin Folsom, and Judith Rane.

** Before the March ended there were several regular publications: *Peace City News, The Paper, The Peace March Update, The Lampoon.*

after 15 or 20 miles of walking in the desert extremes of hot and cold and wind. Struggling with zippers on tents also took time after a day's walk. The desert dust was playing havoc with the interlocking plastic teeth on the device that was essential if Marchers were to have privacy in their tents and protection from rain, insects and snakes. In time, Dick King, who had retired from the Coast Guard, and his wife Dorie devoted themselves to full-time work keeping tent zippers, as well as the tents, in good repair.

The big kitchen trailer could not negotiate some of the turns on Powerline Road, so some Marchers struggled to prepare food that had been brought to camp by small vehicles using one of the infrequent roads that led from camp to the highway. On a particularly hot day, Don Wright, a loyal and imaginative March supporter, appeared in a four-wheel-drive pickup with a load of ice cream—enough for everyone. Don was to turn up without warning again and again during the March, always with some welcome surprise, the most important of which was a pumper truck. Many different people wanted to help the March or take part in it. About a thousand applications had never been acted on, and some of these applicants were clamoring to be taken in, now that we were once again in motion. But the Board of Directors decided to delay accepting more new Marchers until it could be sure it could take care of those already involved.

Marcher Darryl Purpose, hoping to form a band, combed the March while it was in the desert, looking for other musicians. He took those he found to his condo in Las Vegas where they were joined by other musical Marchers already in the city. There they created songs and practiced together. At one point, most of the female musicians decided to set up a separate group—Wild Wimmin for Peace. The others, including one woman, formed Collective Vision. The two groups performed many public concerts as the March proceeded and continued to give concerts long after it ended.

On the afternoon of the tenth day of walking along a dirt road, a huge turreted building loomed ahead like a mirage—Whiskey Pete's Casino just on the Nevada side of the California border. Marchers set up camp a few hundred yards away on BLM land in California. Then dozens rushed for the lavish, cheap meals that Whiskey Pete's, like all Nevada casinos, serve to lure in the prospective gamblers. Telephones, real bathrooms and other amenities drew Marchers like

Star Wars has nothing to do with defense. It is a blatant attempt to regain absolute superiority through the development of new, offensive weapons.

–Dr. Robert M. Bowman, President, Institute for Space and Security Studies

41

magnets. More than one of us took a room there, offering the comforts of showers to dusty companions. Whiskey Pete's management was torn between welcoming our business and throwing us out.

During the desert trek a very busy supporter of the March was 55-year-old Joseph Broido, a Harvard-trained economist who had been a consultant to big corporations. He had a knack for finding the right people for jobs that had to be done, and he understood how businesses had to be run if they were to do what they had set out to do. But he did not anticipate one source of income that developed the second night on the California-Nevada border.

While the City Council was in session about 11 p.m., a man appeared, laden with bundles of money, each counted out to contain $18. Walking through camp he gave one of these packets to every astonished Marcher he encountered. Someone thought of encouraging the recipients to donate to the March all or part of this windfall, and soon a bucket was full of one, five and ten dollar bills. It finally contained $1,800, with which the March was able to buy a tractor to haul equipment. But who was the mysterious donor? And why $18?

The man's name was Michael Sherry, and he explained that he had been lucky at the gaming tables nearby. He didn't need the money he'd won, so he gave it to the March. And $18? In the Hebrew language the same word stands for both 18 and life. Sherry would again become our benefactor as we shall see later.

After the rest near Whiskey Pete's, and delays because of the uncertainty of obtaining a promised site in Jean, Nevada, it was time to set off again. In the hope of getting some media attention, Marchers put on a ceremony when they officially crossed, as a group, into Nevada. (We had, however, been walking back and forth between the California camp and the restaurant in the Nevada casino from the moment we arrived.) After drawing a line in the dust, where they supposed the state line to be, people lined up along it and all at the same time took long strides into Nevada shouting, "California!...Nevada!" This was the first border crossing ceremony. It was to be repeated 15 times with Marchers calling out the names of all the states they had crossed.

An additional part of this first ceremony was the presentation of a huge Marcher-baked cake to the amazed California Highway

Whiskey Pete's had a great breakfast —three eggs, home fries and toast for 95¢. There was a trucker at the lunch counter. We talked, mostly about why we were marching. When he got up to leave, he pushed crumpled up dollar bills into my hand and said, "I've got kids. You keep going."

—John Light, Marcher

Patrol officers who had been with the March all the way. The cake was accompanied by many words of thanks for their help. People being nice to cops!

At the last camp before Las Vegas, peace activist Daniel Ellsberg gave a vivid report of how he, with others from Greenpeace, had just penetrated almost to Ground Zero at the Nevada Test Site. The party had gone in at night, hoping by their presence to prevent, or at least delay, a test that the administration had announced it would make—and which represented a rejection by the United States of the Soviet offer to continue to refrain from testing if the United States would do likewise.

Some Marchers had already demonstrated at the gate to the Test Site, protesting the resumption of testing, and now many more would go to the gate at the time of the next test. There they helped swell the demonstration to the largest number it had reached up to that point. Eighty Marchers, acting as individuals, stepped into the forbidden site, were arrested and served up to two weeks in jail. While GPM demonstrators were present, the second test was twice postponed. The GPM never sanctioned civil disobedience, but those who chose to disobey the law nonviolently were respected by everyone on the March. Tolerance for the ideas and ways of others in Peace City became a lesson in acceptance, and finally a hallmark of the March.

The Marchers looked forward to Las Vegas with great hope, not because they had illusions about winning at roulette, but because Las Vegas was a city, the first since Los Angeles, where they would be met and seen by fair numbers of people—and the nation would, through the media, become aware that we were on the road to stay. Also, Las Vegas might produce money. Big-talking promoters had promised thousands of dollars from concerts and fund-raising activities, but these events did not materialize. Several groups of Marchers worked at cross purposes in the city, and there was a great deal more activity than accomplishment. In hindsight it was clear that a body so wary of central controls could not manage to direct the energies of those Marchers who wanted to rush on ahead, each doing his or her own thing. But how to strike a balance between spontaneous creativity and planned efficiency? Peace City was not the first community in the world to stumble around as it tried to solve this problem.

Las Vegas was not a complete loss, however. Although actor

Again and again, generally in secret from the American public, US nuclear weapons have been used…in the precise way that a gun is used when you point it at someone's head in a direct confrontation, whether or not the trigger is pulled.
–Daniel Ellsberg

43

Robert Blake did not hustle nearly as much money as he expected, he did attract some media attention to the March. While Marchers were having a rest day in camp at a park at the edge of town, several dozen local citizens came to a potluck dinner at Peace City.

Marchers, though forbidden by ordinance to solicit funds on the Strip, were allowed passively to carry collection cans there, and they got a few dollars in the cans, some from casino employees. But the people who daily wagered millions in the gaudy casinos put their money only on the gaming tables and in slots.

In Heritage Hall, a Black community gathering place in North Las Vegas, we heard the voice of Rev. Jesse Jackson who spoke by phone from Missouri. Jackson called us the "soul of the movement," and he maintained connection with the March from that point on, boosting morale.

Phil Schulman, a young seminary student and Marcher from Berkeley, California, had worked long hours to stage a peace fair at the University of Nevada. When only a handful of students showed up, Phil felt his efforts had been in vain. But a year later, when he was attending a demonstration at the Nevada Test Site, he met a young woman who had been one of the few who attended his peace fair. She had been so moved by the March that she organized a university student peace group, members of which were with her at the Test Site demonstration.

One rough spot in Las Vegas turned out to be the safe placement of Marchers in private homes. To obtain invitations for us to shower and sleep and eat in Las Vegas homes, some unknown Marcher had issued publicity over a local television station asking people to offer hospitality. Offers did come in—one from a man in whose home another local resident attempted to rape a woman Marcher; another from a man who dealt dope around the clock and threatened his male guests with a pistol.

After this the Marcher-in-the-Home planners were cautious about indiscriminate publicity. From Las Vegas on, hosts for Marchers were obtained mostly through churches and other organizations that could vouch for the people who were offering overnight facilities. Marchers looked forward not only to welcome showers and meals, but also to the fellowship of families and being able to communicate the anti-nuclear message on a face-to-face basis. Marcher-in-the-Home also let many ordinary citizens be a vital and intimate part of the drama.

If Las Vegas was difficult in one way, Utah promised to be difficult in another. Many citizens of Utah tended to regard any opposition to governmental policy as unpatriotic, and more specifically Utah officials supported the nuclear arms policy of the administration. When news reached the office of the Utah Department of Transportation that PRO-Peace had collapsed in the Mojave Desert, a celebration took place, according to Bob Goff, an active March supporter. People in the office of the governor were relieved, in contrast to the helpful attitude of the governor of Nevada. Peace Marchers, these officials assumed, would not be crossing Utah–Hooray!

On a more practical level, officials had reason to be concerned. Boyer Jarvis, vice-president of the University of Utah and an ardent March supporter said, "There is a long stretch of I-70 [the proposed route across the state] with nothing, no water, nothing. The state officials saw the March as poorly equipped, underfinanced and naive. Their worry was that [they'd] have to rescue the Marchers at great expense to the state."

Once it became clear that the GPM was indeed headed for Utah and that the governor's office was bent on stopping it at the border, March supporters in Salt Lake City kicked into high gear and made use of an umbrella peace organization called Utahans United, which claims many leading citizens as members. Attorney Tim Dunn called together a few fellow members who met weekly in his office trying to work out a plan agreeable to Marchers as well as to state officials. Dunn was also preparing a lawsuit that claimed it was unconstitutional to deny us the right to walk through the state.

At the same time, Bob Goff began to shuttle back and forth between the March and Salt Lake City in an attempt to effect a compromise. Of his first approach to the governor's staff, Bob said, "I was told that the March was not coming through Utah and I was ordered out of the office." He later learned of a governmental plan to meet the GPM with the National Guard at the border. Not a man to give up easily, however, Bob continued to act as a mediator between the March, Utahans United and government officials. On one trip, he presented to a meeting of all the Marchers a proposal that Salt Lake City supporters felt would probably satisfy the state

Niles went back to his youth and spoke about when he was 17 and lived 18 miles north of the Nevada Test Site, in a small mining town. He used to watch the mushroom clouds in the morning. Then he rolled up his sleeves and showed me the radiation scars that had remained since his youth.

–David Gray,
The Paper

45

officials and would also allow the March to make up some of the time that had been lost in Barstow. The plan involved bussing Marchers north to Salt Lake City from a point in southwestern Utah and then southeast across the state to I-70 near the Utah-Colorado border.

"We [supporters in Salt Lake City] were hearing from Bob Goff that the Marchers weren't thrilled with our heretical notion of not walking all the way," recalled Boyer Jarvis, "but there seemed to be enough acceptance so that we could continue discussions with our contacts in state government." With seemingly unlimited patience, Bob Goff continued to negotiate until a plan was agreed upon.

April 14, 1986: Marchers react with shock to news of US jets bombing Lybian targets.

When we neared the state line, Lillie Baiardi, March coordinator for Utah, found herself faced with a different set of problems. Dozens of people began to stream through the southern part of Utah asking for donations, a place to stay, showers, meals. At her home in Springdale in southern Utah, Lillie received many phone calls both from Marchers and from unhappy citizens who were being solicited by people who said they were advance Marchers. Some of the invaders really were advance people, but many were apparently freeloaders taking advantage of the expected arrival of the March.

Arrive it did at the Utah border on April 21. There were no officials to welcome it, but neither was the National Guard on hand. Some unexpected surprises lay just ahead. The first night in Utah found the Marchers hosted by the Shivwitz Band of Paiute Indians, who not only gave them a place to stay on their land but also barbecued hamburgers and laid out a lavish spread of other food for their guests. All this from a very poor group of Native Americans.

In St. George, a day's walk away, the owner of the new Green Valley Resort, who had happened to see the Marchers on the road in California, opened his facilities to them, and everyone reveled in the luxury of swimming pools, hot tubs, showers, jacuzzis and a cooked-to-order breakfast.

The Board of Directors took advantage of the respite from walking to deal with a problem central to the entire March enterprise—the problem of defining in detail the purpose of the March. A statement of purpose was considered, then referred to the City Council in an effort to get expanded input, but discussion continued among people in camp.

Arguments did not revolve so much around the content of the Statement as around the method by which it had been adopted. The complaint was that the Statement came from our governing bodies and not from a general meeting of the March as a whole. A very vocal segment wanted nothing to issue from the March unless it had been drafted and approved by the entire membership. Before long, an unauthorized, shortened form of the Statement was printed and passed out in leaflet form as an explanation of what the March was all about. True to GPM style, this provoked new disagreements. However, for the remainder of the March no one ever spoke out against the general spirit of the Statement or any of its specific objectives. (See Appendix B for text of statement.)

Meanwhile, not all the citizens of southern Utah were being agreeable. The editor of the St. George newspaper, *The Spectrum*, wrote that a certain group of Utahans, which claimed dedication to the Constitution, liberty, morality and truth, accused the Marchers of not supporting America or freedom. "It links the marchers to communism and other left-wing causes and says they foster anti-American sentiment." But, the writer continued, "On the most part Utahans will sit passively by and watch the marchers from a distance."

With few exceptions, this proved to be true. St. George, although it was a community hard hit by effects from above-ground nuclear testing in the 1950s, all but ignored the parade through town. A young high school reporter from a nearby community told Marchers that the local sheriff had warned residents to lock their doors, shut their windows and leave the dogs loose outside: Peace marchers were coming to town!

Accompanying the March in the early weeks was 59-year-old Caroline Killeen. Before joining the GPM she had crossed the country on her bicycle, planting peace trees in more than 20 cities, and she continued her tree planting as she walked, pushing her bicycle along the March route. Later, in Utah, she gave up her role as Marcher, preferring perhaps to pedal, but the tree planting was continued by Marcher Imke Bomer, who was born and raised in Germany. To get free trees for planting, Imke went to grocery stores, tree nurseries, the Forest Service, college botanical gardens and private people (a young man once dug a sapling from his yard and gave it to her). She even attended a tree symposium in Nebraska to create a network of suppliers.

47

The March opened up a whole new issue for the children. It was the first time they had been exposed to an idea that was different from that of their parents.

—Sue Bassett, teacher of one-room school in Boulder, UT

When Marchers were camped in Cedar City, Utah, Mayor Robert Linford wanted to present the key to his town to Peace City during a rally at the local park. Marcher Diane Clark, the "litter lady," was at City Hall to make arrangements about litter pickup just as the key presentation was being discussed. She was asked to accept the key in the name of the GPM.

At the next opportunity, Diane—in her guise as Peace City's ceremonial mayor—would give the local mayor a key to Peace City. This simple exchange of keys and the planting of a peace tree became an important and non-threatening way to involve city officials and local citizens in March activities. Finally Diane and Imke combined the key exchange with the planting of a peace tree—and the Keys-and-Trees ceremony was born.

One morning in the Utah desert we were called together in a circle to learn of an automobile accident. Marchers Win Mattingly and Cynthia Carlson had hitched a ride in the back of a pickup truck for a side trip to Zion National Park, and the truck overturned. Win was seriously injured, and Cynthia was killed. Marchers stood in stunned silence while Cynthia's picture ID was passed around the circle, and people who had known her spoke a few words. It was a shocking, sobering day. The young man who drove the truck later joined the March for a day.

The death of 74-year-old Abe Boxerman, a very active and beloved Marcher, saddened us some time later. He had returned home to Los Angeles for treatment of heart trouble and had died following bypass surgery.

On April 30, the compromise worked out by Bob Goff and others from Utahans United began to be implemented. A group of 50 Marchers set off on foot across southern Utah. The Utah Department of Transportation had reluctantly agreed to let this small contingent walk as private citizens having no official connection with the March. They would cross that part of the state over which the main body of Marchers would be bussed. To maintain the integrity of the March, the fifty would be walking "in the spirit" of the March, and they became known as Spirit Walkers. They planned to cover a grueling 20 to 30 miles a day, and they agreed to rejoin the March in Colorado 19 days later. They were allowed to borrow March tents and they were given food—much of it dried—from the March stores. All their supplies and gear were carried in private vehicles.

Arriving at their first campsite in the late afternoon, the Spirit Walkers discovered that a trucker, who had seen them on the road, had left eight ripe watermelons for them. This was but one example of spontaneous and unexpected support they encountered in a sparsely populated section of the state.

Lacking kitchen facilities, they cooked over an open fire. Two birthdays took place during the 19-day walk, and Dwarka Bonner invented an underground Dutch oven and managed to bake two cakes to celebrate the occasions.

In the meantime, the larger contingent of Marchers walked north to the small town of Cove Fort. There on May 3, private autos picked them up and drove them to Salt Lake City where they took part in a rally at the state capitol. There were a few speeches and Collective Vision put on one of what would be many concerts.

Mike Mertens, 25-year-old Marcher and college student, came to the capitol and explained the significance of a kerosene lantern that had been carried by hand all the way from Los Angeles, preserving a war memorial flame that had come from Hiroshima. Mike was a member of Asian and Pacific Americans for Nuclear Awareness, an organization responsible for keeping the Flame. Here and many times later along the route, new lamps would be lit from the Hiroshima Flame to burn on, keeping alive the memory of the civilians who died when the first nuclear weapon was exploded.

In Salt Lake, Marchers engaged in a practice that would become part of all future public gatherings of the March. Holding hands, they formed a great circle on the State House lawn. Then they went off for visits to homes that had been arranged for them by Una Stevenson through the local churches. Several non-Mormon religious centers took part in this hospitality, and at least one important Mormon, the superintendent of Salt Lake City schools, invited Marchers into his home. Next morning, Sunday, in the Mormon Tabernacle, to which all Marchers were invited, he sat next to one of the authors of this book and commented on what a good experience he had had with his guests.

Everywhere in Salt Lake City, the Marcher-in-the-Home program went off smoothly. In some homes Marchers were teachers of their hosts; in others they were learners. For example, they heard the story of one hostess in Salt Lake who had been a psychiatrist for

I have an 8-year-old who is very gung-ho about war. The March being here gave me an opportunity to discuss the other side of the issue with him.

–Geraldine Zarate, Librarian, Mesquite, NV

the Veterans Administration, but quit her job which consisted mainly of trying to repair the damage that war had done to young men. Instead, she turned to working full time in the movement against war which she found was the cause of much of the mental illness she had been trying to cure.

Sunday morning, many Marchers spoke in churches about nuclear disarmament—a type of outreach that became more and more important as we moved eastward.

It is hard to imagine what would have happened to the March without the untiring support of many Utah residents. Would it have changed its entire plan and followed a route to the south of Utah? Would it have camped on the Utah border and refused to move? Would it have challenged the authorities and entered Utah anyway, risking confrontation by the National Guard? Or would the Marchers have sifted through the state as individuals planning to reassemble in Colorado? Because of intense activity of Utahans United on behalf of the March, these alternatives did not have to be faced, and we moved forward—mostly in busses.

With the problems of Utah behind them and the relative success of Salt Lake City to encourage them, Marchers entered Colorado full of hope. The experience of surviving the California, Nevada and Utah deserts; of being able to move the camp 15 or more miles every day; of finding ways to feed 500 people three meals a day; of generating enough grassroots support to keep it all going—of all this Marchers were justifiably proud. The almost uninhabited desert areas through which they passed had given them breathing space in which to master the logistical skills necessary for traversing the country. Outreach into communities could be postponed, allowing time for preparation and training, until there were communities to reach out to. Colorado would provide fresh opportunities for meeting more people.

Many towns on the proposed route had been contacted in 1985 by PRO-Peace which described a march of 5,000 people who would arrive in need of camping space and water—an overwhelming prospect for any small place. The next communication usually came from the GPM telling city officials when to expect the Marchers, but with no mention of the number to plan for. When 500—not 5,000—friendly and orderly people arrived and began picking up litter along the highways and in the parks, citizens breathed a sigh of relief.

Three days' walk east from the Colorado-Utah border is Grand Junction, a town at the base of the Rockies. Because of the large number of Marchers who came from Colorado, many expected the entire state to be supportive of the March and its goals.

The welcome given Marchers by Grand Junction was cordial but reserved. Susan Rose, a graduate student, said, "In this community the peace movement has had a bad reputation. It's a fundamentalist town, and it carries over into their political thinking. There was hostility toward the March ahead of time." But by the time the Marchers arrived the attitude changed tremendously, according to Susan.

A parade and rally held in the downtown mall drew an estimated 300 people with another 100 joining the Marchers on their swing through the town. A reporter from Denver's *Rocky Mountain News* wrote: "Local reaction to the march has been friendly, though many residents of this predominantly conservative area don't believe in the March's goals." The local newspaper, the *Sentinel*, gave us front page coverage three days running. Susan Rose felt, however, that the impact on the citizens of Grand Junction was on a personal rather than a political level.

Nevertheless, Grand Junction offered a chance to participate in some outreach. A follow-up evaluation done by a team of Marchers gave good marks to the speakers who went into the local schools and to the Marcher-in-the-Home program. Less effective, according to their findings, was the relationship established with the local peace organization and the ability of the March to draw local citizens to GPM events. Members of Citizens Action for Peace, the one peace group in town, felt "overwhelmed and uninvolved" in their contribution to the GPM. The inability of the March to adhere, at times, to a rigid schedule and the lack of attention to local input caused problems. Finding ways to attract local people to March activities continued to be a challenge up to the very end of the March.

No sooner had Marchers left Grand Junction than they were faced, once again, with a stretch of highway too dangerous to traverse on foot, this time because of construction through 20 miles of DeBeque Canyon. Only a token group of ten would be allowed to walk. A different solution was found when, a few miles up I-70 in Glenwood Canyon, a similar situation came up. This time an

If you guys can put me out of a job, that would be great.

–US Army Colonel, talking with a Marcher

51

Climbing up to Cottonwood Pass in Colorado

alternate but very demanding route existed, and 52 volunteers slogged through two days of rain and mud over Cottonwood Pass to preserve the integrity of the March.

To some, the idea of having to board a bus for a few miles of dangerous terrain was no big deal. The goal of the March was, they argued, global nuclear disarmament. The goal was not to walk every step of the way. To others, however, it was indeed a big deal. How could a group, which relied on walking across the country to draw attention to its message, maintain its integrity if its members climbed on busses whenever some state official claimed it was unsafe walk? The issue was hotly debated. The compromise of having a symbolic group walk over troublesome areas satisfied most Marchers, but a handful of people insisted on walking every inch of the way, regardless of police orders or March agreements. The Utah Spirit Walkers had agreed when starting out that they would be shuttled from the Colorado border to rejoin the March, but about half that group changed their minds and walked 25 to 30 miles a day through western Colorado in order to catch up with the GPM outside Denver. Their audacity was admired by many, once they showed that Spirit Walks could be accomplished without incident.

The western slope of the Rocky Mountains along I-70 is dotted with small settlements, many of them old mining towns hoping for a new economic base. The March progressed through these communities as it headed toward the Continental Divide. Despite the lackluster receptions in some places, Marchers found the beautiful mountains and the cool air adequate compensation. And from time to time unexpected hospitality did appear. For example, the resort town of Vail, which had very little suitable camping space, opened up enough condominiums to billet the entire March.

Several of us spoke in a private school in Vail, and others spoke in schools in the surrounding area. A local disc jockey had broadcast daily coverage of the March as it made its way toward Vail, and he continued to do daily reports until we passed Denver. As Marchers walked the highway out of Vail, the mayor, Paul Johnston, and Peace City mayor Diane Clark, led the procession.

Enough interest in peace issues was generated by the GPM within the small permanent population of Vail so that a local Marcher, Pam Telleen, was successful in starting a peace group there after the March was over. The group, the Peace and Action Express, attracts 30 to 40 people to its weekly meetings, an impressive accomplishment for a town that's known mainly for skiing and *après*-ski.

From Vail, Marchers climbed over Loveland Pass, at 11,992 feet above sea level the highest point on the cross-country route. For a weary group that felt all but forgotten by the media, it was a glorious day. As we rounded the last bend before the summit, we suddenly saw dozens of people waiting for us. Television camera crews and reporters were there to record the joyous celebration of a real achievement. Then, with flags flying and spirits high, we began descending the eastern side of the Continental Divide toward Denver and the Great Plains.

Rivers of mud ran through the camp at Red Rocks during a downpour a few days later when we set up our tents in the foothills west of Denver. It was here that singer and veteran activist Pete Seeger made the first of several visits to the March. His words and music cheered the soggy group that crowded into a town hall tent to hear him. The next morning, with the rain still falling, Colorado Congresswoman Patricia Schroeder came and spoke words of encouragement.

As we approached the state's largest city—and the largest since Los Angeles—a letter came from the Colorado organizers: "We feel

Today the only way to achieve genuine national defense for any nation is for all nations to give up violence altogether.

—Jonathan Schell,
Fate of the Earth

confident that Denver will be the March's greatest welcome. Activities already scheduled include numerous benefit concerts, houseparties, rallies, and speaking engagements. The culmination of these events will be a parade in Denver on Friday, May 30th, a rally at the capitol on May 31st, and a Marcher-for-the-Day program on Monday, June 1st." This was heady stuff. However, again reality did not quite match expectations, although there were surprises: public radio gave generous coverage and a shoe company donated cartons of brand-new sneakers.

A noontime parade through downtown Denver stopped traffic, but brought out few spectators. The rally at the capitol the following day attracted 3,000, but at the same time 75,000 were attending the popular People's Fair a mile away. "The March does not draw in the average citizen merely by its presence," was the sober conclusion many Marchers reached.

If there was a feeling of disappointment about the size of the turnout at the rally, it was partly overcome by a totally unexpected contribution of $25,000 from Dr. S.Y. Wang, a Colorado Springs physician. To our great delight, this elderly man walked out on the steps of the capitol to make his very practical gift. Other income brought the GPM treasury up to $100,000 by the time we left Denver. This was a greater surplus than we would ever again have before November 15.

Outreach in the community did increase in Denver. Marcher-in-the-Home and Marcher-in-the-Church programs were well received. Talks at schools got enthusiastic response. Through these

Crossing the Continental Divide 12,000 feet above sea level at Loveland Pass, Colorado

Peace City in Denver

experiences we were learning that we should place more emphasis on taking the March story straight to the people. It was not enough to parade down streets or to expect visitors to come to a public meeting. Perhaps a parade created some curiosity among those who saw it, but Marchers had much more impact when they met citizens individually. One-on-one relations with people encountered on roadsides, in homes and churches, bars and stores, became very rewarding. Curiosity about life on the road led to lively, thoughtful interchange on nuclear disarmament.

But communication of a different sort posed continuing difficulty. The ever-moving March had no telephone and at times it could not keep to an announced schedule. This meant that organizers had trouble planning meetings to coincide with our arrival. In addition, some peace groups felt that their own efforts at fund-raising would be interfered with by the massive demands the March made.

When we walked out of Denver, 300 area citizens joined us for the day, each paying $15 for the privilege. Guests and veterans exchanged news and views as they passed elegant homes where the

*May 30, 1986:
A courier delivers
to Peace City
a Blue Peace
Ribbon signed
by Colorado's
Governor
Richard Lamm.*

residents showed little interest in the procession. Interaction was more lively in northeast Denver, a predominantly Black community. This was a pattern to be repeated again and again in cities: vacant suburbs contrasting with supportive ethnic and working-class neighborhoods. The day ended a few miles out on the plains where busses picked up the Day Marchers for the trip back to Denver.

Chapter III

Life On The March

Wake-up call
Morning routine
Packing up gear
City mode and country mode
Joys of walking
Dinner in Peace City

By the time we left Denver on May 31, most of us had mastered the demands and necessities of camp life and had settled into a routine similar to that of any working person. But instead of the ringing of an alarm clock, the first sounds of the day might be those of a flute, a gong or singing voices designed to coax Marchers out of the sack. A more urgent summons followed a few minutes later with a morning report—the length of the day's walk, the destination, a weather forecast and, at times, other necessary information. "Good morning, Peace City. Today's walk is a distance of 22.3 miles. Rain is expected in the early afternoon, so pack that rain gear. Our destination is Sterling, Colorado. Rise and shine, Peace City!"

Although the wake-up call usually came two hours before the departure of the March column, there was little time to spare. Standing in the first line of the day gave people time to read—or to hear someone read—communications posted on the porta-potty doors, which served as bulletin boards. The posted material might be the latest poem or petition or protest or farewell letter or word of praise for some task well-performed.

Next came a rush for the water tank, which had been fitted with faucets and a drain trough connected to a big bladder holding graywater which was later pumped into a tank on a pumper truck labeled "Non-Nuclear Waste." After hand washing, teeth brushing and, for some, shaving in cold water, lines formed for a stand-up breakfast that might be anything from oatmeal and pancakes to last night's leftover beans.

Then we hurried off to pack up sleeping gear and tent and to put unneeded clothes in one of the hundreds of green milk crates that served as storage boxes. The crate (everyone originally had two) and other gear bore the tent number of its user—it might be OY8. The letters once stood for orange town, yellow village; but these PRO-Peace distinctions became almost meaningless as the town and village system evolved into something more informal.

Morning rituals at the hand washing trailer

Each Marcher had two crates for personal possessions in a gear trailer.

Before departure, each of us put his or her crate into a big trailer, then piled tent, sleeping bag and pad on the ground in rows, according to the letter prefixes, near the trailers. After the day's march began, others who remained in camp to work would load up all this gear for transport to the next site. In order to move the gear, feed Peace City, wash the dishes, schedule speakers, contact the media, find future sites, screen new Marchers, keep the vehicles running, teach the children, and do the hundreds of other things necessary to keep it all going, we were expected to work two days a week at a self-chosen job. This not only provided for day-to-day operation, but it also gave young Marchers valuable on-the-job training.

On non-work days we walked—or were supposed to. Some walkers started the day alone or in groups of twos and threes before the main contingent left camp; others straggled sometimes miles behind. Although this was not the pattern in the first months on the road, more and more people resisted attempts to get everyone to walk "behind the flags." The "free-walkers" argued that marching in a column was pointless in rural areas where few people saw them. Besides, if they were free to stop at the local cafe or farmhouse, it was possible to do more outreach with the few local people they did encounter. The behind-the-flag supporters felt that the March should present a unified image— that TV and newspaper shots of a mere handful of people following the flags was a misleading and detrimental picture of the GPM. Although the issue was never completely resolved, the City Council passed a compromise resolution that approved of people walking ahead of or behind the main body in rural areas. This became known as "country mode." In more populated districts we would form a column behind the flags and this, of course, was designated "city mode."

However Marchers got themselves down the highway, everyone welcomed the 12-mile stop where a pickup truck laden with do-it-yourself lunch ingredients pulled off to the side of the road and lunch workers set up serving tables. One could expect some of the following: peanut butter, bread, hot dogs, cold boiled potatoes, raw or cooked squash, jicama, hummus, tuna salad, and an occasional treat of baked goodies or fresh fruit.

The porta-potty trailers, which had accompanied the March all morning, making stops at approximately four and eight miles, stopped at the lunch site, too. If the walk was a long one there would be stops at 16 and, if necessary, 20 miles. The vision of tall, blue porta-potties parked on the far horizon heralded the next welcome pause in the miles of marching.

To be able to spend several hours a day walking across our country was a rare treat. Difficult though it could be at times, most of us found walking the easiest and most pleasurable part of the March. Morning was usually the best time to be out on the road. We were rested then and temperatures were usually moderate, especially in summer. Small things, which go unnoticed as we travel by car, became objects of fascination as we walked. Birds, butterflies and other insects, weeds and flowers captured our attention. Horses found *us* particularly interesting. They would watch us as we approached, then dash off in a spirited gallop and return to stare at us as we passed by. Sometimes Marchers up ahead would leave something in the road for the rest of us to see. More than once, we found a discarded glove in our path, its greasy fingers placed in a peace sign.

Being able to observe the world slowly and at close range gave us a connection to nature and a deeper appreciation of why we were walking—of how closely we are connected to all living things. Sleeping and walking on the earth changed us as we walked to change the world.

The weather figured much more prominently in the lives of most of us than it ever had before. We got drenched when it rained, huddled in our tents during electrical storms, searched out small bits of shade on sweltering days and shivered in our sleeping bags when dew froze on our tents. And when the sun was out and the temperature was in the 70s, it was glorious to be alive.

Each of us carried some kind of water container as we walked, and the March monitors reminded us over and over, particularly in the desert, to drink plenty. The pickups hauling the porta-potties carried cambros of water (15-gallon plastic containers with spouts), and at each rest stop we could refill our canteens. It was not unusual for us to drink a quart every four miles.

Walking together provided the opportunity for getting to know one another. We shared experiences, dreams, fears, gripes, hopes, laughs and tears. We automatically smiled and flashed a two-fingered peace sign at passing motorists and locomotive engineers, and they frequently waved back.

Diversity in the way we walked, as in almost every other phase of March life, was obvious. Some of us read (aloud or silently). Others talked, chanted, drummed, sang, pulled a wagon, pushed a bicycle, hauled a baby or picked up trash. Alternatives to walking were rollerskating, jiving to music (real or imagined), running, race walking, skateboarding, bicycling and one man—our clown, Hinton Harrison—even rode a unicycle.

Now and then we would come upon some gracious farm family or neighborhood resident who had set up a card table with paper cups and cold water or lemonade on their front lawn. Often it was children who waited with drinks which they shyly offered us. Their hospitality was as refreshing as what they served.

In Colorado we were joined by Rev. Katsuzo Sawada, a Buddhist monk who walked while beating a drum and chanting. By the time we reached the East Coast, four more monks from the same order were walking with us. Dressed in saffron robes and carrying a long purple banner with Japanese characters, the monks called attention to our procession. Initially, some Marchers complained about the noise of the drum. One Marcher even took Sawada to mediation. After the mediation session, Sawada and the complainant emerged arm in arm, smiling—and the drumming continued. Eventually, those who were bothered by the drumming learned to walk some distance away from it. Others of us found the rhythm helpful in creating a meditative frame of mind.

The GPM would have increased its impact on Iowa City if it had been more attuned to the city's feelings and walked in a column.

*–Martie Olsen,
GPM coordinator
for Iowa*

61

It is false to talk of peace while possessing weapons destined to take life. When we talk of peace, we must lay down all murderous tools.

—Buddhist Chant

Rev. Katsuzo Sawada, Buddhist monk who chanted and beat his drum from Denver to Washington, D.C.

On most days, we arrived in mid-afternoon at the new campsite where we tracked down our tents and sleeping gear arranged in piles segregated, more or less, by tent numbers. After picking a tent site and creating a new home for ourselves, some of us might flop down for an afternoon snooze. Amazingly, some people after walking for most of the day still had energy to engage in the contortions of hacky-sack or a strenuous frisbee game. Others explored the nearby town, went to one of several meetings in session or accepted the ultimate challenge of locating the occasionally available shower within walking distance and arriving there before all the hot water was gone.

Dinner was served any time from 5:30 on, with lines for vegetarians, non-dairy vegetarians and meat-eaters ("omnivores") forming outside the kitchen as much as an hour before a meal was ready. The evening fare varied more than the other meals, but rice with veggies or beans or tofu was a frequent entree. After eating at some nearby spot on the ground, we pre-washed our own dishes in a soapy tub. Dishes and utensils were then all re-washed in a specially equipped trailer by the dishwashing crew that also cleaned up the pots and pans. (See Chapter IV for more detail about the kitchen and dishwashing.)

Evening hours were a time to read or write—usually by flashlight and propped up in a less-than-comfortable position in the tent. But there were also sundry meetings or an educational event to attend or a video about some phase of the peace movement to watch on the small camp TV, which was powered by a gasoline generator. (And once in awhile in this nonviolent community the *Rocky Horror Show* was played on the video.)

Some of us wrote poems, such as this one by Frank Sahlem:

Sewing by Candlelight

On a starlit morning early in Autumn
    I am preparing for a walk.
There is a hole in my sweatsock.
And there is strife among nations,
      because what God has joined
        men have put asunder.
Will we raise enough dust today
      to fill in the break among nations?
Can we build a bridge in our lifetime,
      that can carry the weight
        of our failure to understand?
Do we have a lifetime left?
I count my blessings and set to work.
      The needle moves in and out.
Orion lies on his side. A rooster shouts.
      A stitch in time saves the world.

Think about the time you woke up to find the condensation on the inside of your rain fly playing water torture with your face. How about that exotic oatmeal you had for breakfast; ah, that smoky western flavor! Then there was the time someone opened the gump on you because s/he didn't hear you say "occupied."

Cynthia McGarvie,
Peace City Lampoon

People also socialized with friends, worked on journals or songs or letters, caught up on sleep, or called home, if a phone was nearby. Most Marchers developed an eagle eye for public telephones, and it was rare to see one without a cluster of people waiting nearby to make a call. When we camped near a population center, at least a few of us had the opportunity to participate in a Marcher-in-the-Home evening that usually meant a hot shower, a bed and sometimes an offer of the host's telephone. And, of course, a sharing of experiences with the always curious host family.

Once a week the March had a rest day, which everyone hoped would provide a chance to wash clothes. On one rest day after Denver, a local laundromat owner welcomed Marchers and, when a downpour went on and on, let them spend the night in his laundromat basement. In another town, we encountered a rare display of hostility when the laundromat owner refused to let us use his washers and dryers. The original PRO-Peace plans had called for a laundry truck which would have had facilities for washing clothes. The scaled-down GPM had no such luxuries, but real necessities were provided by various March departments.

More than 30 of these departments, staffed by volunteers, divided up the task of keeping us on the road and bringing our message to communities through which we passed. An account of how they functioned appears in the next chapter.

Chapter IV

How We Did It—Nuts and Bolts

Getting there
Communication
Trucks and tractors
Mealtime
Cleaning up
Management and money
Community interaction
Education

Day-to-day progress along the road resulted from the work of March volunteers in many departments—Day March, Sanitation, Kitchen, Peace Academy, Sites, Routes and Permits and about 30 more, representing vital functions of the Great Peace March. Sites, Routes and Permits, for example, had an advance team that went out daily looking for potential Peace City campsites the size of two football fields and flat enough to have room for about 200 small dome tents, three big tents, a kitchen, refrigerator truck, dishwashing trailer, food storage trailer, an assortment of other trailers, three sets of towed porta-potties, busses and trucks, plus a variety of small vans, sedans and motor homes. The tasks of all the other departments were just as demanding in their own way, and yet almost all of the volunteers who staffed them walked, in addition to handling their ongoing chores.

Not every department is described here, because of their sheer number, but what follows will give some idea of the challenges and how they were met by Marchers themselves inside our movable Peace City.

● *Sites, Routes and Permits*

PRO-Peace had attempted to find appropriate campsites all across the country. But for one reason or another the GPM could use almost none of them. So it was necessary for an advance team to scout out the best roads and to secure camping space.

Three women, B.J. King-Taylor, Angie McCarrel and Wendy Camack volunteered for the job. B.J. was formerly a police dispatcher in California, Angie a college student, and Wendy an artist. From Barstow on they constantly shuttled back and forth between the March and the communities ahead along the route.

In the beginning, and through the Midwest, they often dealt with private landowners who could give them a site. Occasionally an owner might say: "I guess it's okay." But as the March moved eastward it began to take days and weeks to work through the bureaucracies, because sites were usually in city or county parks, and vast amounts of paperwork were often required.

Dan Chavez, the GPM's lawyer, worked with the department and helped get the necessary camping permits from city, park and other officials. The fact that the GPM could not afford liability insurance made his job seem at times impossible, but his arguments—and his charm and gentle persistence—almost always prevailed.

Half a dozen times the March had to post bonds ranging from $1,000 to $5,000, but all were refunded. Princeton University demanded a personal waiver signed by each Marcher. When we got to camp no one ever asked for the documents.

While we made our way across the desert in California, Nevada and Utah, we often camped on land owned by the United States government and managed by the Bureau of Land Management (BLM). Alden Sievers, mentioned earlier, was the area manager for BLM land in the Mojave Desert around Barstow, and his decision to allow the GPM to camp on the land he oversaw was crucial. Not only did he give us his permission, but he also compiled a 16-page document about the March which he sent to every BLM office in areas where he thought the March might be staying. Part of the document was a handwritten letter in which Sievers said, "I have gained great respect for [the Marchers'] dedication and their willingness to cooperate. They are just nice folks....They have also treated the public lands with tender loving care: campsites have been left cleaner than when they arrived, and flagging was put around little creosote bushes to keep them from getting crushed!" This assistance and commendation by Sievers early in the reorganized GPM helped the advance crew in their very difficult job all along the way.

Rather than working far ahead in some areas, B.J. found it more successful just to drive around a town. "Somehow," she says, "we would be pointed in the right direction.

"I knew what we needed, and we *had* to get it. There was a lot of detective work involved—finding a piece of land, going to the nearest house, asking...who owned the property, determining who was the best person to make a decision. Then I'd say, 'Look, we're going to be here in two days. You have to do something!'

"Sending polite letters ahead to bureaucrats didn't work. That only gave them time to bar the door."

Cautious site owners were assured they did not risk much by providing space. What if our vehicles left ruts? We promised to fill them in and we did. Would tent stakes leave holes in grassy areas? Such holes actually aerated the soil, we told them. As for trash control and cleanup, we had a nearly unblemished record.

"We called the local police ahead of time, told them we were coming and asked for their help," Angie says. "We needed help, especially at difficult intersections, and information about possible restricted areas such as bridges and some types of roads."

I called the ranger at Lake Manawa to see what kind of crowd to expect. He said, "You'll never have anyone treat your park better."

–Steve Keith,
Concessionaire,
Lake Anita, Iowa

67

Finding sites and getting permits were only part of the department's job. The team had to determine the best route from one camp to the next, then give the information to the GPM's mapmaker. Guy Colwell, an artist, did all the maps until we reached Omaha. Then he began training others to help, and from Chicago east, four people shared the job.

Guy would start to study a route as soon as it was selected. Then he rode along it with a driver to check highway and street names and to calculate mileage. After coordinating that information with state and county maps, he sketched the route.

Often Guy had to make one map for Marchers and a different one for vehicle drivers, because walkers did not use the freeways and our vehicles often did. His biggest problem was getting accurate information. He learned to check for freeway offramps and to make sure the trucks could get under the overpasses and around obstacles.

In the beginning, Guy sketched his maps in ink on white paper and then had them photocopied. As more and more copies were needed, he drew directly on stencils and ran off about 150 on the March ditto machine. Forty to 50 maps went to drivers of trucks, tractors and support vehicles. Fifteen to 20 were given to our CIA (Community Interaction Agency) so it could let local people know our route and site. The remaining copies were for Marchers—especially those who walked alone or in small groups and might easily get lost.

- *Day March*

Headed by Laura Johnson who had volunteered for the job in Barstow, the Day March department was responsible for getting the Marchers themselves from one campsite to the next. She and three others were the Day Officers, called DEMACs (derived from *Day March Coordinators*) who took turns leading the column out of camp each morning. But there was more to their job than that.

A day ahead of the March, a DEMAC rode over the proposed route checking the mapmaker's information, paying particular attention to details important for walkers. Where were the sidewalks? Where was a good place to cross a highway or street? Could we walk on the shoulder of a highway? Where could the porta-potties be parked for a rest stop?

Non-violence... does not mean meek submission to the evildoer, but it means putting one's whole soul against the will of the tyrant.

—Gandhi

Next the DEMAC got in touch with the local sheriff and police or state patrol and told them how many people would be walking the next day and whether they would be walking in a single column or in many small groups. Often, Laura says, she was met by a stonyfaced chief of police. But after she showed him a letter of recommendation from the Nevada State Police, he usually relaxed. Sometimes she could talk with him about peace and children and grandparents and the reason for the March, and she would leave with good feelings on both sides. Those interviews, Laura believes, were one of the reasons we had such good relations with the authorities all along the way. But they took time, and often Laura got back to camp too late for dinner.

Responsibility, however, was nothing new to her. She had grown up in a poor family, one of ten children, and her deaf sister was with her on the March. After going to college on an art scholarship, Laura lived for a while near a community of Amish people whose peaceable ways influenced her. She was working as a horseback guide on a ranch when she heard about the March, took off to join it and was trained in Los Angeles as a March monitor. So she volunteered for the head DEMAC job when we walked out from Barstow.

Monitors in the Day March department carried two-way radios which kept them in touch with the DEMAC who was leading the March and with the communication vehicle, Comm II.

The DEMAC for the day set a walking pace of three-and-a-half miles an hour in easy terrain, of three miles an hour in cities, and in bad weather or difficult terrain, whatever speed Marchers could manage.

After the DEMAC came four flag carriers. They carried the United States flag, the flag of the state in which we found ourselves at the time, the United Nations flag, and the "World Unity" flag made by Marcher Dwarka Bonner. This was unique to the March. It depicted the double helix of the DNA molecule superimposed on an image of the planet Earth on a blue field. Betty Phelps, who had once run for Congress on an anti-nuclear power ticket and got 40 percent of the vote, often helped to carry banners and signs that proclaimed the March's message.

From Utah to western Pennsylvania, Marcher Josh Silver was in

The GPM is "the largest semi–permanent floating protest game in the United States."

–Michael Lansberg,
The Globe and Mail
(Toronto)
November 1, 1986

charge of the flags which he kept stored under a truck. Part of his job was to find volunteers to carry them. To pass the time while he was walking, he and a friend often chatted in a new kind of pig Latin Josh had invented.

It took a fair amount of strength to carry a flag, even with a belt that helped support it, and windy days were very difficult. Marchers had a special respect for Felix Loera whose congenitally crippled foot did not keep him from bearing a heavy flag day after day.

● *Comm I and Comm II*

A 1974 Chevy van, Comm II (meaning communication), accompanied the March column. Comm I was a stationary unit. Both vehicles were equipped with CB and two-way radios. A radio operator in the van with the Day Officer and the driver maintained contact with local authorities and with the DEMAC and the monitors who had walkie-talkies. By Nebraska, all the radios were in bad shape, and buying new ones was a constant theme in budget discussions.

Comm II carried emergency medical supplies, ice and extra water, in case anyone needed help. The driver tried to stay in visual range of the March column, but she or he also scouted out the route if there was some doubt about how to proceed. If there was some hazard ahead, such as a house being moved down the highway, the radio operator warned the DEMAC.

Lana Vining, the driver in charge of Comm II, once said, "It's probably the only motorized vehicle to have gone across the country at three miles an hour."

Comm I was the communication center for the March. At one time or another it had been housed in a motor home, a van, in the bus owned by Bob Alei, a former high-school teacher, and finally in a beatup, right-hand-drive bread truck. Sam Wolfe, a retired high school science teacher, frequently operated the two-way radio, CB and ham radio equipment inside, and he taught several Marchers all they needed to know to become operators.

Sam sometimes used the ham equipment to contact families and friends of Marchers. Once he called an ambulance for Doug Friz who fell over a tent stake and injured his back at 4 a.m. on his way to a breakfast shift.

Comm I stayed in camp till all other vehicles moved out, then went on to the next site. From its stationary positions it kept in touch with other March vehicles as well as with local authorities.

Already in bad shape, Comm I lost a wheel one day going down the highway past the March. Fortunately, no one was hit, but the mishap left several more dents in the truck. Its roof leaked, too, and Sam had a hard time keeping the radio equipment dry. Once he hooked the aerial to a porta-potty that was then hauled off, taking the aerial with it.

- *InfoCenter*

Often called InfoComm, this was a small trailer where Marchers picked up information and where rumors were often dispelled or confirmed. There volunteers composed, typed and duplicated the *Peace City News* every day. Marchers who wanted to put a notice in the paper dropped their written material in a slot on the side of the trailer, and it would appear (usually) the next day. Daily route and site maps were also issued from InfoCenter as were some of the other March publications.

Two large bulletin boards hung on the outside walls of the trailer while it was parked. One held information about Peace City—the daily schedule, the route map and where to find laundry and shower facilities, when these were available. On the other, people posted clippings from newspapers and magazines about the March and topical peace issues as well as fliers about happenings outside Peace City.

A table often set up by InfoCenter held handouts, forms for camp activities and whatnot. (The porta-potty doors were used for posting political and editorial communication among Marchers and latest in-camp humor.) InfoCenter volunteers, often Dave Gray, a college student from Minneapolis, and Carlos de la Fuente, a municipal judge from Los Angeles, were on hand in the afternoons to answer questions and help people find information.

- *Transportation*

Coleen Ashly had been the PRO-Peace transportation supervisor in charge of moving the city. That meant organizing the drivers, making sure they had vehicles to do their work, sending vehicles off

Despite public statements about "deterrents" and "defense," the true nuclear policy of the Pentagon [is to use] nuclear weapons to threaten, fight, survive, and even "win" a nuclear war.

–Michio Kaku

71

in an order that would allow them to leave camp and park in the next one without blocking anything. When PRO-Peace folded, Coleen simply continued as before. Eventually, she was appointed to head up Transportation for the GPM.

In Barstow we had only a few vehicles, but many people went home to get their vans or trucks. So did Coleen and her husband Dennis, and their small trailer became the transportation office. Bob Trausch brought his van which was used as the support vehicle for families, hauling children, food, water or whatever else was needed. Marian Anderson and Madonna Newburg brought their VW camper which became the Blister Bus. When Marchers' feet gave out along the way, the Blister Bus, or some other private vehicle, such as the Weary Wagon, would pick them up and deliver them to the next camp.

Most of us were unaware that the March left Barstow without a water truck, a key vehicle for a desert crossing. The Transportation department had been assured that we could fill our cambros at our next site in Yermo. But when our pickups got there, permission was rescinded. Luckily, a private landowner allowed us to fill the cambros from his well.

In those early days, three people might spend the entire day looking for water. Finally, the City Council decided to rent a water

Sometimes we jury-rigged showers. A few times local firemen came to camp and sprayed us with their hoses.

Grownups didn't have all the fun getting clean.

truck for $500 a week, and we used it until Rifle, Colorado.

Marcher Dave Miller, who liked to say he came from a long line of Texas horsetraders, did most of our vehicle acquisition. In Rifle, he struck up a conversation with a gas station owner. The man listened to Dave with great interest and asked what he could do to help. Dave told him, "Our most important need is a water truck."

"Really?" the man replied. "Come with me." Behind the station stood a lovely one. Its owner rented it to us for $500 a month. He paid two March drivers $100 a month each so he could legally insure them, and he paid for the truck insurance, too. From then on, the drivers would fill that one truck with municipal water, paying for it at residential water rates, and that would last us for several days.

Ed Trunck, a retired fire captain, left the March at one point. Later he returned to our campsite in Rabbit Valley, Colorado, and brought us Aqua Too which he had designed and built. It was a flatbottomed trailer with a big water drum in the center and several hoses with faucets surrounding it. We could not only fill containers from this tank but could also wash there. Aqua Too was with us the rest of the way.

Transportation also arranged for people to go to scheduled speaking engagements, to a doctor or hospital and furnished shuttles to showers and laundry facilities. Until the children got their own busses, Transportation arranged for vehicles to take them on field trips.

All of this demanded a daily schedule to coordinate available cars and drivers. The coordinator, called the Sender, made sure each driver remembered his or her assignment and would show up at the right time. The Sender also helped make decisions about the order in which vehicles left camp. In bad weather, the gear trailers had to leave early to reach the new site before Marchers arrived, so they could get to their dry clothes quickly. Children who needed transportation had to be counted before and after a trip. Replacements had to be found for cars that were disabled or for drivers who were walking instead of working.

"I never had a sense I was in the least bit in control," said Sender Patricia Riley, who had been a Spirit Walker in Utah. "But like magic everything was moved every day. No one knows how." Patricia was on leave from her job in administration at UCLA.

● *Maintenance*

The Maintenance department was staffed by two journeymen mechanics and two, sometimes three, apprentice mechanics with two or three years experience. Dale Porter and Michael Laemmle were the journeymen, and they took on full responsibility for keeping our vehicles on the road.

The Maintenance bus, an old Los Angeles urban transit coach, had been donated by a Ford dealer in Barstow. It had not been running for two years, so the men took out the engine, rebuilt it, made the bus into their workshop and kept it going all the way to Washington. In addition, we acquired a service truck equipped to repair vehicles that had broken down on the road.

All major March vehicles were pre-1974—one Chevy truck was a '49—so they all had to be nursed along. Finding parts was a nightmare. Much of the work was frustrating because some volunteers did not know how to use equipment properly.

Each morning, mechanics and drivers had to make sure all the vehicles could get started. People often damaged the brakes' air lines between tractors and trailers, using them as steps, so brakes had to be specially checked. Trucks and tractors were not always

On verification: One US satellite now makes it possible to tell which newspaper a man on a street corner in Moscow is reading.

—Science, December, 1985

driven by the same person, and the big machines responded temperamentally to being handled differently: they often broke down.

The kitchen needed "an infernal amount of time." Nipples on the stove burners were not meant for the fuel the March used. It took a while to discover this. Some people didn't know how to work the generators; they might crank them until the batteries were dead, and some didn't know that diesel fuel needs to be preheated.

Problems came in bunches. Once, three school busses all needed new steering units at the same time. Then water pumps went out; next it would be the brakes. The worst problem was finding reliable machinists along the way to make those parts that could not be bought. Sometimes, the men spent days until they finally found someone who could do the work.

The tractor called the Blue Bird, which a supporter had lent to the March, had been sitting in a backyard for a year and needed to be completely rewired, a major piece of work. Then in Chicago our mechanics had to rebuild the engine. After the March, it was returned "in better shape than when we got it."

The men once figured out that they spent at least $50,000 on parts during the March. Repair shops calculate that parts are one-third of the cost of a job, with the rest for labor. At this rate, our mechanics donated $100,000 in labor.

The men worked very hard. It was a seven-day-a-week job, sometimes for 18 or 20 hours. No rest days. No walking. They often got tired and emotionally drained. But they knew that without them the March could not go on. Often, they couldn't even have dinner with the rest of us, because they were out on the road getting vechicles "pasted together." Sometimes when they came back to camp there was no food left. Eventually, in Grand Junction, Colorado, they put their own little kitchen in their bus. A continual complaint from some Marchers was that the mechanics drank beer. They said they were used to it and "no beer, no work." And so a compromise: the Maintenance bus usually parked some distance from other vehicles.

In St. George, Utah, while everyone else was playing at the resort, the mechanics did a valve job on a 4-wheel drive vehicle.

Found—a teddy bear in my car at Phillipsburg site. He's enjoying the novelty, but seems a bit homesick. Shall I drop him in the mail to you, or what?

—Gary Wilson,
Peace City News

Then they replaced an engine in another truck and put brakes on one of the tractors. As they worked they could hear people laughing and having a good time next door. Still, they made their own good times. The bus often had a casual party atmosphere. But one of the best moments was getting to the point where they could listen to an engine, feel for a problem and talk through what had to be done. The respect Michael and Dale had for each other's competence and artistry was remarkable.

Dale had gone to Canada during the Vietnam War, "for ideological reasons," he said. When he heard about the March, he filled out an application for a job with PRO-Peace, but was turned down. Later he learned that the March was in trouble. So he quit his job, loaded his tools into his own truck and drove to Barstow. He said he "felt in his bones that the March must not fail and that he would be needed."

Michael was working on yachts in Marina del Rey, California, when the March started. He, too, applied to PRO-Peace and was told that a mechanic had already been hired. Art Hoag, the first mechanic, did much to get the vehicles that came to Barstow in running condition, but became exhausted and discouraged and left at the Nevada line. Michael joined Dale at the Whiskey Pete's site.

- *Moving the City*

Drivers of big vehicles had to have a Class I license, but co-drivers might be in training. Drivers worked closely with Maintenance. After a thorough morning check of their equipment, all the drivers met to coordinate the move of the day: Which tractor would pull which loads, which truck needed to be serviced, what were the road conditions? Double loading (one tractor pulling two trailers) was prohibited in some states. What were the rules about double loads in this particular area?

At times, drivers knew they were doing something illegal, but there might not be any option, so they'd do it. At some weigh stations officials just shook their heads when a driver couldn't produce a registration or permit. The documents might have been applied for but not received, because mail didn't always catch up with Peace City. Police were usually sympathetic. Driver Brian Goldman says he doesn't know of anyone getting a ticket.

Even after the coordination meeting, plans often had to be changed. A truck might get stuck in the mud or have a mechanical breakdown. The following, says driver Chris Broadwell, the father

I didn't think about the issue [of the arms race] much before the March was here. I pushed it aside. It was too uncomfortable.

—Gwen Phillips,
South Bend, IN

of two other Marchers, was not an unusual day:

"We connect the tractor to our trailer, crank up the feet, lift the pad and find it's broken. So we disconnect the tractor, put down the feet; then we scout the whole length of camp to get Maintenance. We put our tractor onto another unit and pull that to the new site. When we try to go back to the old site to pick up another load, we find ourselves blocked in our turnaround by the Anarchy bus. We spend 25 minutes to convince them to move their bus eight feet so we can get out. We return to the original site, reconnect our unit, start moving and get hung up on a large tree root. The wheels begin to spin. We stop, connect ourselves with a chain to Dale's pickup to get pulled out, but nothing happens. Donna comes back with her tractor, so we connect that tractor to ours. That doesn't work. We disconnect Donna, drive her back to Maintenance and she gives a jump start to the Maintenance bus. We hook that bus up to our tractor. The chain breaks, and we are still stuck. Finally, we disconnect the double trailers to which we had been connected, and we pull out one unit. We disconnect it, put its feet down, go back, get the other unit, connect that, pull it out and put it on the road. Then we connect the two units, lift the feet, put the pads away, connect it up, and we are at the new site before dark."

Donna Kreycik had succeeded in getting her Class I license while she was on the March. She now owns and drives her own tractor-trailer rig. On a typical 20-mile day, a driver would make three trips to the next camp and put 120 miles on the odometer. During the last months when the vehicles were in bad repair something was wrong almost daily. All the air systems had developed multiple leaks by the time we hit the East Coast.

The coordinator for the day handed out maps before drivers left for the next campsite, discussed problems with them and gave them money for fuel. It took $60 to fill up a tractor—between $20 and $30 a day for fuel.

Once out of the campsite, it was "map time," but maps were sometimes inaccurate. Drivers often used their CB radios to get help from other truckers on the road and to find fuel for the kitchen. The CBs were turned on all the time, and a constant chatter went on

The summer solstice will be celebrated all day and night at Cottonmill Lake Amphitheater. At 3 p.m. there will be a "herstoric" Watermelon Ritual which dates back to someone's active imagination.

–Peace City News, June 20

77

between March drivers and truckers.

Brian Goldman, who had been a firefighter with a crash and rescue team in the Air Force, had a keen understanding of the danger Marchers faced when they walked three abreast or pushed carts or skated down the highway. They didn't know how difficult it was for truckers to see them, especially in the rain when there was a lot of spray. Because of his worry, Brian often joined the Marchers. "Walking with others," he says, "gave me an opportunity to creatively convince people to stay off the road without infringing on their freedom."

At each new site a Marcher called a Receiver directed the drivers. Some Receivers understood how our big rigs worked, but one asked a driver to move his sideways six inches. Another didn't see why double trailers couldn't be backed up. (They always hinge in the middle.)

While mapmakers suggested a plan for positioning vehicles in their spots at a new site, Receivers worked out the details. "You had to go to the site early to study it," says Receiver John Darrah, one of the Anarchists on the March. "Eventually, you'd get a picture in your mind. You'd actually construct the camp in your head."

The first decision was often where to put the kitchen. There had to be room for the bladder, which stored graywater. This enormous container lay flat on a level spot downhill from the kitchen and connected to it by a hose. The back of the dishwashing trailer needed to face the kitchen, as did the dry-food trailer. Ideally, the main vehicles formed a circle, so that there could be a sense of community—a place where people could congregate and where small serving tables could be placed. (Marchers didn't sit at tables; we ate standing up or wherever we could find a place to sit.)

The gear trailers needed to be as close as possible to the tent sites so people would not have to walk too far for their tents and sleeping bags. Two sets of porta-potties were parked near the tents and one near the kitchen. Comm I and InfoCenter had to be central and next to each other, if possible. They and the kitchen were the hub of Peace City. The Post Office, Finance, Peace Academy, the Community Interaction Agency busses and the children's busses parked where space permitted.

July 8, 1986: Marchers consume 45 gallons of ice cream donated by the ministers of Oakland, IA.

- *Campscape*

A striking feature of Peace City was the three large Moss tents that served as town halls—indoor space for meetings, performances and storage of gear in wet weather. These orange, blue and red town halls gave a kind of carnival look to our camp, and were a nighttime refuge for some Marchers who chose to sleep inside. Campscape volunteers were in charge of putting up, taking down and repairing these big tents. Theirs was a fairly easy job except during bad weather. The center pole had to be dropped during high winds and electrical storms which might come up during the night.

Each day a different worker served as supervisor and was responsible for getting the route map to the next site, placing the tents correctly according to the site map and seeing that the tents were put up and taken down. The tents were transported to the next site in a van which the supervisor drove. Usually the Campscape workers helped clean up the campsite after everyone was gone, filled in ruts and did what they called landscaping (hence the name Campscape).

- *Kitchen and Food Prep*

At the Stoddard Wells site, after PRO-Peace pulled out, everybody was asked to join one of several task forces set up to deal with obvious March needs. Dwarka Bonner wanted to get out of the wind and rain and went to the orange town hall tent. There he listened to Jeff Moss, who had been hired as head chef for PRO-Peace, talking about the problems of feeding a group. Jeff said that Marchers couldn't do it all by themselves. For one thing, they didn't even know about the many permits needed to satisfy health regulations.

However, since so many people had no intention of going home, something had to be done. Dwarka found himself on the food task force. He had learned to cook in big quantities when he lived in India for three years.

Sharon Gonzales also joined the food task force. She had had experience in large-scale food preparation when she was doing famine relief work with the Peace Corps in Africa.

These two and other volunteers took on special jobs. Sharon and

Waging peace in this country takes a lot more guts than waging war.

–Ralph Nader

79

Dwarka became coordinators. Jeff Polikoff, who slept in the kitchen, had traveled a lot and had learned to live simply. He assumed the task of making non-dairy food and sprouts. Mike Schwab, a young man from Germany, made yogurt.

There were few really experienced cooks among the volunteers. Those who knew large-scale food preparation had to be divided between the different shifts. Hector Gonzales, who had worked in restaurants in Mexico and Santa Fe, worked on dinners and taught others what to do.

Kitchen duty could be extremely pressured, for between 300 1,000 people had to be fed three times every day. When meals were late—which they often were because of truck breakdowns—hungry folks got upset and some would bang on the kitchen walls and shout through the door. Hector was one who never lost his temper and kept things calm.

At first, the coordinators tried to plan menus for a week, but

The food prep crew cuts up veggies for dinner

donations of food and leftovers which needed to be used up soon made that impractical. If coordinators and/or cooks had ideas for a meal several days in advance, they put labels on whatever they wanted saved. Sometimes, we learned, they hid certain food so it wouldn't be used up before the planned dish could be prepared.

The breakfast crew of four or five started to work between 2 and 4 a.m., and they were the people who also got the kitchen packed up for moving. Pots and pans and utensils necessary for starting supper had to be taken from the dishwashing trailer to the kitchen, just in case it got lost or broke down on the way to the new site. Then everything had to be tied down on the kitchen floor with bungee cords.

The day coordinator, who worked from 7:30 a.m. to 7:30 p.m., came in after breakfast to see what food was on hand and what supplies were needed. He or she helped with packing up for the trip to the next site and with unpacking upon arrival.

Three or four cooks worked on dinner. Barring a hangup, they could be in the kitchen as early as noon.

At each new site, five or six people gathered in the prep tent (later the prep trailer) to peel potatoes for dinner, cut up lettuce (we almost always had a green salad), wash fruit—and in the Midwest—shuck endless donated ears of corn. At one point too few people volunteered for prep duty, and the kitchen crew announced that we would get only peanut butter for supper. Before long, volunteers began to show up again.

The lunch crew came to the prep area between 4 and 5 p.m. to get food ready for lunch the next day. In the meantime, cooks worked in the kitchen.

Late at night the bakers came on. There was a regular crew, but sometimes additional people got inspired to bake. They made delicious things for lunch, and whenever we had a border crossing, they baked incredibly large cakes in the form of the state the March was leaving. These were shared with the highway patrol and police who had assisted us. People from peace organizations and others who met us in the new state also joined, and we all would have a party.

We eat a lot of brown food here. The best way to get me out of bed is when my tentmate comes in saying, 'Hey, we got color on the plates today! Something yellow'.

–Marcher

July 17, 1986: The kitchen staff prepared a meal of Nicaraguan style food. It was Nicaraguan Independence Day.

81

Propane fuel was a big and complicated problem. For some reason, there had to be a separate account for propane purchase, and the stuff had to be transported safely, because it is explosive and under pressure. In New York, we had to get a special transport license to carry it, and the truck driver had to take a test to prove he knew how to handle it.

* *Food Buying*

On Task Force Day, when people volunteered to work in various departments, Kimberly Solerno chose to work in food buying. The job wouldn't be totally foreign to her, because she had been a pastry chef. Her friend Jessica Tracy, trained as an anthropologist, joined her, and the two managed the department all the way to Washington.

Until we reached Denver, buying was somewhat haphazard. It usually started with a search of the Yellow Pages for suppliers of dairy products, canned goods, meat and produce. After placing orders, the team picked up the food and brought it to camp. As we progressed through the Western desert most of our food was donated, so the team bought only eggs and produce. "We had some horrible food those days," says Jessica.

In Las Vegas, the buyers discovered an organization called The Gleaners that collects food and sells it inexpensively to needy people. Some of the food was a little outdated; some came in bent cans—but there was nothing seriously wrong with it. Kimberly and Jessica gave The Gleaners $200 and took whatever they needed.

Food banks also sold food reasonably. Jessica and Kimberly would fill a large pickup with government issue cheese and junk food. Even though the junk food probably wasn't healthful, Jessica says it was good for morale. More people than would admit it really craved the sugar and the familiar tastes.

When we approached a city, Kimberly and Jessica usually called churches and asked how to find a food bank. Often the pastor would go with them and put the order on the church account.

In Denver, they found that former PRO-Peace workers had set up connections with several wholesale food distributors. From then on, these companies were a major source of such things as canned goods, tofu, peanut butter, natural foods, paper goods and dairy

Our meals have a lot of variety and often include recognizable dishes.

–Sharon Gonzalez, Kitchen staff

products. The food team became very good at persuading suppliers to give them restaurant and bulk purchaser's discounts—and to bring orders to camp.

"It was lovely," Jessica recalls, "to see $3,000 worth of food being delivered to our campsite and the delivery people accepting our check."

It was lovely also to receive large contributions. In Wiggins, Colorado, a bakery donated hundreds of loaves of bread. Jessica and Kimberly loaded them into an open pickup truck and drove to camp in one of the worst rainstorms of the March.

In Omaha, the Marchers relished crates and crates of donated blueberries. Later on, farmers brought corn, tomatoes and melons. In Gary, Indiana, people gave us hundreds of pounds of potatoes and string beans. In Toledo, the Natural Ovens of Manitowok donated bread. Both the bread and its bakers were wonderful—they sent delivery after delivery.

What were some of the food team's problems? In the Midwest they felt a lot of pressure to buy from farmers direct, but the process was too time-consuming. Then there were certain Marchers who wanted exotic foods. Items such as seaweed or umeboshi plums were not easy to come by, and they were very expensive as well.

In spite of problems, Jessica and Kimberly did all the major food buying in two days a week and walked on most other days. And with all the donations, plus canny buying, they succeeded in feeding us all for $1 a day each. Some of us got thinner on the March diet, but a few actually gained weight.

● *Dry Foods*

Our dry foods trailer, acquired just before we got to Denver, was the size of a large moving van. At a weigh station it once held 82,000 pounds of rice, beans, flour, salt and other staples. The trailer was so heavy it often sank deep into the mud and had to be completely emptied before it could be jacked up and moved.

During a rainy stretch in eastern Colorado, Darius Broadwell decided he needed a dry place to sleep, so he "elected himself" manager of the vehicle. Before long he started to build shelves along

Common sense tells you that we have enough weapons and don't need to keep building them. But common sense doesn't seem to be a prerequisite for holding public office.

–Mike Metzler, Campbellstown, PA

83

the sides and down the middle all the way up to the ceiling. Then he worked out a method of storing packages so that they took up the least space. He kept this system in his head, but he also wrote down whatever was donated—about 35 percent of our dry food. Darius consulted with the food buying team, listing what was needed and in what quantities. (We could eat up 50 pounds of oatmeal at just one breakfast.)

When cooks said they needed something, Darius always knew where to find it on the shelves. One of his time-consuming jobs was to keep hungry snackers out of the trailer.

August 9, 1986: Marcher Geoff Mercer runs in the Moscow Peace Marathon with 20 members of Athletes United for Peace.

For a while, two or three other volunteers worked with Darius. Their main job was shifting packages around so that the oldest items were in front, and they spent a good deal of time picking up what had fallen from the shelves when the trailer moved from one camp to the next. Cooks had to prepare meals for vegetarians, non-dairy vegetarians and "omnivores," and what was more natural than to call our dry food person "Non-Darius"?

* *Dishwashing*

The Dishwashing department acquired its own trailer in Barstow. The Dishwasher had three sinks—one for washing, one for rinsing and one for dipping dishes into a disinfectant mix. It also had room for drain boards and work counters and storage space for all the big cooking and baking equipment.

Lorraine Heller, on leave of absence from her job at Headstart, organized the Dishwasher's work crews. She found leaders to take charge of both the breakfast shift, from 6 a.m. to about 11 a.m., and for the evening shift from 6 p.m. to about 10:30 p.m. These people were also responsible for packing the trailer at one campsite and unpacking at the next. Bungee cords kept things pretty much in place, and later on, wooden guard strips were installed. This helped especially on winding roads.

Many of the Dishwasher operations had to be developed by trial and error. It soon became clear that dishes and utensils, as well as pots and pans, should be scraped and pre-washed before they went through the process in the three sinks. Dori King of the dishwashing crew came up with a solution which Paul Ross, a boilermaker with a practical and creative nature, helped put into operation. They got two freestanding plastic sinks and set them up outside the trailer where Marchers could pre-wash and rinse the dishes they had just used. Later the department bought more sinks for pre-washing pots and pans after they had been dry-scraped on a table outside the trailer.

Geoff Mercer of the Sanitation department solved another problem: sinks drained very slowly because wastewater ran into the large graywater bladder with a very narrow neck. Geoff suggested bucketing the water into large garbage cans from which he could quickly suck it up with his hose and pumper.

Originally, the only ventilation in the trailer was the door, and the place was like a sauna when work was going on. Bob Powne, Lorraine's husband, bought two windows for $3 each, cut holes in the side of the trailer and put them in. That helped.

Dishwashing could be done by 14 volunteers a day, but having 17 was better, and the job required some strong muscles to lift heavy commercial pots and pans. Eventually, we had seven crew leaders, some of whom went the whole distance to Washington.

Unattractive though dishwashing might sound, it was a popular job in camp. A camaraderie developed among the crew members and several of them commented that they liked it because it gave them time to think their own thoughts.

Volunteers in the Dishwasher were faithful. In New York City many cut short their sightseeing to perform their in-camp duties. Usually, dishwashers were faithful about walking, too. Some signed up because working on the evening shift didn't interfere with marching.

What was the department's worst time? One frosty night late in the fall, the plastic pipes froze and began to leak. All the plastic sponges froze too. The most memorable event? The musical that Lorraine Heller wrote about dishwashers—a big hit when it was performed in camp.

- *Sanitation*

When the March was stalled in Barstow, Geoff Mercer reasoned that we needed three basic things: food, water and sanitation. He volunteered for the Sanitation department because, he said, his

Sign on kitchen:
Oatmeal for
non–dairy only.

Sign on milk:
Milk for
oatmeal only.

85

background as a sheepshearer at home in New Zealand prepared him for "grunt work," which was certainly a big part of his job. Once he commits himself to something, Geoff says, he will carry on responsibly, and he was indeed committed to the March.

Working in Barstow with Mark Wolfe, who had been in charge of Sanitation for PRO-Peace, Geoff learned to take care of waste disposal and the toilets. But first the porta-potties had to be saved. Their owner, who hadn't been paid, wanted to work out a deal with the GPM. The couple who had contracted to pump and clean the toilets every day stayed on for a few days without pay. They were aware of our predicament: without them we would have been stopped immediately by health authorities.

How much money did the department need? To make an estimate, Policy Board member Trevor Darvill sat down with Geoff and Mark, and they came up with a figure—$37,000.

It seemed an enormous amount, but Geoff began telephoning. The Peace Development Fund and the Rockefeller Foundation promised him enough to make a downpayment on the porta-potties. For the next three months the GPM made weekly payments of $1,250, and the toilets were ours.

Next: a pumper truck to dispose of waste. Geoff found one in Los Angeles for $13,500. He and other Marchers put up their own money for a downpayment, but when Geoff went to Los Angeles to close the deal, he found Don Wright, a supporter from Simi Valley, California, waiting for him. Don had already contributed $1,000 to buy a few days' grace for the toilets. Now he and his wife decided to buy us the pumper outright. Geoff drove it off, and it served the GPM every day to Washington.

Having the pumper meant that we no longer needed private contractors who charged as much as $250 a day to dispose of waste. Geoff could now do the job for one-tenth that amount and pump out graywater from the kitchen and dishwashing trucks as well.

Soon after getting the pumper, Geoff spent several of his rest days giving it a new coat of paint, and then Marcher Jerry Conner, who had been a sign painter, helped decorate its back and sides with signs: "Nuclear-Free Waste," "$20 Million a Day for Nuclear Weapons—*That's* Waste!" and "If Nuclear Weapons Are Peace Keepers, This Must Be a Truckload of Roses."

Peace is the most important moral problem in the world today. I can't think of anything more important than what you are doing.

—Father Theodore Hesburgh, President, Notre Dame University in talk to Marchers

The pumper truck that serviced the porta-potties

"The signs helped carry our message across the country with a smile," Geoff said, "which is the best way."

Geoff's most difficult problem was locating municipal authorities who could give permission to use their waste disposal plants. The plants often closed on weekends and holidays, which required a lot of advance planning. Geoff kept telling himself that no matter how frustrating the job was it had to be done, and he became a skilled negotiator. If an official demanded a fee for dumping, Geoff explained that the March didn't have much money and other municipalities had permitted a free one-time discharge. Usually, he got an okay, but if not, he would then call the local police and explain that the health and well-being of hundreds of people were at stake. That worked: the only place Geoff had to pay for dumping was Las Vegas.

Bob Yantes, who became known as "porta-potty Bob," volunteered to drive a pickup truck that towed the toilets. After that, Geoff had only to pump them out and get them cleaned. There were some very dedicated cleaners, but not many. It was not a popular job. Still, a retired military man who visited camp and took a look at the toilets, went to the donations table and made a sizeable contribution. People who kept the toilets as clean as these Marchers did, deserved his respect and support, he said.

For a time, Geoff himself spent a lot of time with a bucket and brush. One day he went to the briefing of the City Council and said, "Anyone who wants to emulate Gandhi can do so by volunteering

87

for toilet cleanup." That gave Gene Gordon, a former radio producer, an idea. Next day on each porta-potty door there appeared an appropriate poem with a picture of a skinny Gandhi, bucket and brush in hand:

> Porta-potty poets don't come here to sit and think,
> I bet you're sure I'm going to end this line with
>   stink.
> No, we look for inspiration, for our goal, you see,
> Is to attain our salvation and emulate Gandhi.
> Mahatma was a lawyer, a statesman and a seer,
> But the lowest toiletbowl cleaner was his peer.
> So be a great soul like Gandhi, you Tom or Sue or
>   Russ.
> Join porta-potty poets and clean this John with us.

People took the hint, and more volunteers began to help.

Eventually two other drivers also volunteered so Geoff could walk more, and the new drivers took over in August when he left temporarily to run in a marathon in the Soviet Union.

• *City Managers*

When the March was stalled in Barstow, one person began to coordinate departments, but soon found it was too much of a job. Early in Utah at the Snowfield site, the City Council decided to appoint three City Managers (CMs), each responsible for coordinating several departments.

CMs made sure that all departments had all relevant information. How far is it to the next site? Will we need an afternoon snack because it is a 20-mile day? Will there be a rally so that Merchandising has a chance to do some selling? Will people be at Marcher-in-the-Home? (The kitchen needs to know.) Do the mapmakers have a vehicle? And so on.

Every Tuesday after dinner, City Managers and all department heads met as an Operations Council for a weekly exchange of information. What will the upcoming terrain be like? What is the altitude (it changes the gas mixture the kitchen needs)? What are security needs, especially in larger cities?

All the energy that had been invested in individual lifestyles and money and the pursuit of success and happiness and relationships shifted toward one common goal— global nuclear disarmament.

–Jonnie Zheutlin, Marcher

Every department had a chance to discuss what impact this information would have on its work. At times, the group had to brainstorm to figure out how to meet challenges. At other times, it might be perfectly clear what each department had to do. Most departments most of the time worked well. People learned to listen to what was important and to adjust.

In rotation, the CMs attended City Council, Board of Directors and department meetings, and they created the agenda for and conducted the All City meeting, which was usually held on Wednesdays. The All City meeting was an important gathering that provided Marchers with information and opportunity for feedback and exchange of ideas. Here people let others know about plans, concerns, wishes, reactions—in a forum where they would be heard.

All departments submitted their budgets to the CMs who then made recommendations to the City Council for its approval of funds and finally okayed the payments through the Finance department.

The CMs did not supervise departments, nor did they have anything to do with choosing heads of departments, although they would make recommendations.

When there was a conflict between departments, the CMs tried to mediate and work things out in the spirit of "reasonable people will behave reasonably when spoken to with reason." On an easy day the CMs still might be able to join the walk at noon. Many times, however, it took all day to work out snags and find people who needed to be involved in solving a problem.

The CMs became highly respected Marchers and, since none of them abused their power or forced their own opinions, they had the ear of every faction from the Board of Directors to the Anarchists.

All the CMs made outstanding contributions to the March and to the success of the department. To mention just two: Buffy Boesen was the eldest of eight children. Living in a large family and then in a religious community had accustomed her to working out problems cooperatively. Peter Talbert, a racewalker and one of the Utah Spirit Walkers, brought to the March his experience as a teacher and counselor and an understanding of the forces that move people.

Ultimately, we believe...that the struggle is not between different national destinies –between opposing ideologies–but between catastrophe and survival. All nations share a linked destiny; nuclear weapons are their shared enemy.

–Dr. Bernard Lown

● *Security*

The Security department, later re-named "Peacekeeping," faced an ongoing dilemma that made its job difficult. Some Marchers saw the need for a strong security presence; others resented what they thought was militaristic behavior on the part of Security workers. Both factions complained frequently, and Barbara Cone, who headed the department from Ohio to Pennsylvania, learned to say: "I hear your concern. What proposals do you have, and what will your part be in the solution? Which shift will you work?" (Barbara had worked in a school for disturbed adolescents. "After that," she says, "I could handle any child or adult tantrum on the March.")

It was often difficult to get people to volunteer, because many Marchers differed so much in what they wanted for the department—and because some had trouble remembering they had signed up. Therefore, many of the regulars often worked more than one shift. Shifts lasted for three hours each, starting when the March came into camp and ending at breakfast time.

Peacekeepers had three different kinds of jobs: Rovers walked through camp to keep an eye out for troublemakers. Their work was made difficult by Marchers who believed peacekeeping included tolerance for even the strangest and most threatening of visitors. In the words of Freda Weis, a former Air Force security person and an early Security department head, "The Rovers were a visible deterrent, especially if they kept an irregular pattern of roving."

Then there was Gate Security. These Peacekeepers often were the first Marchers the public met. They greeted visitors and helped them orient themselves in camp. The Peacekeepers also helped Receivers park vehicles. A very important part of their job was trying to keep out people who might cause problems in camp. This was not easy, because camps were wide open places. Along the way, several people who caused trouble had attached themselves to the March, and in two instances the local police had to be called to help remove them.

Lastly, the Security Day Officer supervised Security operations and, if it was necessary, made emergency decisions.

Two in the morning could be a busy time. Outside Pittsburgh someone threw a cherry bomb into the porta-potties at about that time. The Security people linked arms to form a blockade, then

Barbara stepped over and talked to the hecklers. What did they know about us and why we were walking? She got them to discuss the March with her, and finally they left camp.

Another night some people decided they needed to do some "primal screaming." Although they thought they had gone out of earshot, they could be heard clearly throughout camp. Barbara thought it sounded as if "they were being cut up." But when she confronted them, they were crestfallen and later wrote an apology to the camp.

Barbara Cone resigned in Pennsylvania. She felt burned out from trying to keep work schedules filled with responsible people and with dealing with the many safety concerns of the campsite. Others continued to work, however, even though challenges persisted as the March grew and went through the populous cities of the East. Although less of a cohesive force than before Barbara's resignation, Peacekeeping functioned and nothing catastrophic happened.

At the Randall's Island site in New York City, the Peacekeepers dealt with urban predators and one or two blatant thefts, and they had the respect of the New York Police Department officers assigned to the site. In Washington, several volunteers took charge of Security and were present night and day, even at the Tacoma Park, Maryland, site following the official end of the March. Like so many Marchers, they found themselves taking on a task they could not have imagined doing before they joined the Great Peace March.

● *Finance*

A converted school bus, painted white and blue and called Fisk 'n' Disk (from Fiscal and Computer Disk), was headquarters for the Finance department. In the beginning, Judith Rane served as Chief Finance Officer, and Carole Schmidt was head of the department. Judith, a long-time peace activist, was a former wrangler, a potter and a computer systems analyst. Carole, who had worked as a political campaign manager, was already familiar with a life of constant change. By the time she was 13 years old, her family had moved 13 times.

On the road, the March worked almost completely on a cash basis. This meant we sometimes carried along $10,000 to $15,000 in actual currency, mostly small bills. On Sundays people from

March weather report: 40 percent chance of showers today; 30 percent chance of laundry.

departments that had budgets came and picked up their cash for the week.

Our home bank account—the main repository of our funds—was in Los Angeles, and we also had accounts in local banks on our route. The Los Angeles office would wire money to whatever bank we were dealing with at the time. We could then draw on that account for the cash we needed. The only things paid for by check were major food orders and some equipment.

"Banking wasn't difficult when we were in a state with branches throughout," says Carole. "We just changed branches as we moved ahead. We also tried to deal with banks that had a somewhat 'correct' political outlook."

July 27, 1986: Marchers Karen Anderson and Jim Smith are married at Peace City's Coralville, IA campsite.

A few banks flatly refused to deal with the March and it was a good bet that, if a crisis was going to arise, it would choose Friday or the day before a holiday, when banks were closed. Yet the department always managed to find the cash for emergencies.

The department people included a day accountant and a duty finance officer. The day accountant was responsible for cash counts, morning and evening, and a witness was always present. These two volunteers had office hours in Fisk 'n' Disk and kept records of all department budgets and receipts on a spread sheet. (Receipts confirmed the data on the spread sheet.) Once a week, receipts from each department were reconciled with the money allocated to that department.

Carole Schmidt, Judith Rane and others set up our initial accounting system in Barstow. Mike Cone, a CPA hired by the March, refined it. Before the GPM had any bank account outside Los Angeles, Carole slept with as much as $15,000 under her pillow.

Whenever Dave Miller set out to buy a vehicle, such as a trailer or tractor that might cost several thousand dollars, people in Finance would count out the cash, give it to him, and he'd be gone on a five- or six-day vehicle-hunting trip.

In Barstow, the department once had $6,000 in cash allocated to the purchase of a gear trailer and lease of a water truck. The owners of these vehicles wanted to be paid by check, so Carole needed to get the money to a bank. Prudently she decided to ask the security people for an escort. "The guy on duty asked me how much money I was carrying and I told him," Carole remembers. "He opened the public address system and shouted out that Carole had $6,000 on her and wanted an escort to go with her to the bank."

Finally, the department bought a safe that could be locked in the Fisk 'n' Disk bus; now Carole didn't have to sleep with money under her pillow any more.

Judith Rane made the department's final report after the March ended. "We were scared to death," she says. But a businessman Marcher who was familiar with the department's records and activities said he had never encountered an organization in which financial affairs were handled with such honesty and integrity.*

● *Mayor's Office*

After the March left Utah, mayors of towns along the way began coming to visit Peace City. What we needed, City Council decided, was someone to greet officials and show them around. Diane Clark, who had been the Greenskeeper (litter lady), was asked to do the job. She refused. She didn't want anything to do with politics. Some people then circulated a petition: *Diane Clark for mayor of Peace City*. It would be a community relations job, not a political one. On a vote of five to one the City Council approved the idea.

Diane redefined her job frequently. What she wanted most was to have many people involved in many interactive events in the communities along the route. Often she asked "real" mayors what she ought to be doing. The mayor of Lincoln, Nebraska, told her she should go to an upcoming World Mayors' Conference in Chicago. She asked City Council for funds, and they agreed. At the conference she introduced herself as mayor of Peace City and spoke about our purpose. She received a standing ovation from the other mayors.

Charges that the USSR has violated past arms control treaties are either largely unsubstantiated or arise from ambiguities in the wording of the treaties.

–The Defense Monitor, 1985

---

* The total receipts handled by all those in charge of March finances amounted to $1,018,987.40. House-to-house canvassing by Marchers brought in $76,502.94 of this amount. Total grants by the Peace Development Fund came to $90,805. Payments by new Marchers totalled $53,910.55. Events brought in $22,787.76. Sale of merchandise netted $59,288.72. There were other miscelaneous sources of revenue including gifts of $10,000 or more from four individuals. Most of the donations were in small amounts and there were 19,000 of these.

The March began to get some of the community members involved in ceremonial ways– ways they hadn't expected.

–Bob Anderson, Lt. Gov. of Iowa, after attending a Keys–and–Trees ceremony in Newton, Iowa

94

One of Diane's important functions was officiating at Keys-and-Trees ceremonies which were held in city parks, at city halls, schools, retirement homes and campsites. Marchers were encouraged to attend these interactive ceremonies; some read poetry, some sang, others just mingled with the crowd to foster a peace dialogue between Marchers and citizens. In the Adopted-Son-or-Daughter program a Marcher acted as the son or daughter of a particular community and promised to write once a month to city officials, reporting on our progress across the country.

At one of the early Keys-and-Trees ceremonies, Bill Pettijohn noticed that the Peace City key was made of foil-covered cardboard. He had some redwood in his bus and decided to cut and varnish a wooden key. Then he carved a wooden plaque to commemorate a peace tree planting ceremony. After that he and Sonia Hughes, a medical researcher, made more than 200 plaques and more than 500 keys.

Bill had worked as a cross-country trucker for 30 years, and he says there isn't a rig made he hasn't driven. A man of many skills, he worked in the Transportation department, was one of the electricians who kept the kitchen going and built tables and pigeonholes for the March post office which he installed in part of his bus.

Donna Love, mother of four grown sons, and Shelah Notkoff, a dance therapist, served the mayor's office as an advance team. A few days ahead of the March, they visited a community, met with people in the city offices and set up an official welcome and the Keys-and-Trees ceremony. Back in camp, they enlisted Marchers to participate in these activities.

Three or four people worked with Mayor Diane in her mobile office (a 1976 Dodge van where she also slept). Every day, one of the secretaries wrote letters thanking people for hospitality and for a variety of gifts—keys to the city, caps bearing a town's name, medals and other mementos. Tyler Divis kept an inventory of gifts: what they were and where they were stored.

A typical day in the mayor's office began with a staff meeting at 7 a.m. to organize, divide up and assign the work. Then people took down their tents, had breakfast and by 8:30 a.m. started to work. Often work went on in a city library or at a local city hall to arrange advance bookings. Work continued until lunch, either on the road with the March or in a cafe along the route. After lunch, the staff sorted, filed, typed and prepared for ceremonies in the next town. In the evening, Diane sometimes went to a workshop, discussed problems with others or just spent time alone.

- *Medical*

What to do about inevitable medical problems? After the hypothermia episode at the bitter-cold site on Stoddard Wells Road, the decision was made to provide nursing, screening and first aid help. But there would be no official March M.D. in the Medical department which was headed by a registered nurse, Clare Cattarin. Nurses did the basics for which they were qualified but for anything major they would call on local physicians. Two Marcher physicians, Larry Heiss and Dick Edelman, did see patients for minor problems from time to time. The main problem with having an official March doctor was that he or she would have to be licensed in every state we passed through.

Before we reached Washington, three Marchers had appendectomies, all done in local hospitals. A number of broken bones, allergies, throat infections and pulled ligaments were treated by doctors along the way. In numerous places, the Medical department asked Physicians for Social Responsibility for names of doctors who might cooperate. Only a few refused to help, and about 70 came out to camp or set up clinic days in their offices when the March came through. A dentist in Philadelphia cleaned Marchers' teeth one whole day (see Chapter IX).

On average, 100 people needed some sort of treatment each week, mostly minor. We went through 10,000 aspirins, three cases of bandages and ace bandages, several boxes of antibiotics and many bottles of antihistamine.

The department's biggest problem was the few people who had little idea how to take care of themselves, such as those who walked repeatedly without shoes and got glass splinters in their feet.

The very competent staff of seven or eight volunteer registered nurses and LPNs came from the United States, Indonesia and Australia. Toward the end of the March, a physician's assistant helped out. Each staff member worked two days a week. At first, they had two-way radio contact with Comm I, but the equipment was stolen. After that, the nurse on duty at night simply told Comm I how to locate her tent in an emergency.

Daytime headquarters were in a little white trailer with a big red cross. It opened early in the morning before we left camp. By about 10 a.m. all headaches, earaches, stiff necks, blistered feet and sore throats had been taken care of. At the next campsite, office hours were from 4 to 6:30 p.m. But if a nurse heard that anyone needed special attention, she made a housecall to that person's tent.

● *Media*

Almost as soon as we woke up on our own at the Stoddard Wells site, we knew we had to deal with TV, radio and newspaper people. They would be coming to us; often it would be useful to get to them.

Elizabeth Fairchild and Chris Ball created the new Media department in Barstow; Bill O'Neill and others joined them sometime later. Elizabeth had done public relations for a community in California; Chris, a newspaper reporter, had been on his college frisbee team. Bill had had a brief career as a reporter on the *National Enquirer* and was a marathon runner. They operated out of a tent the first couple of months, and Elizabeth still chuckles about sitting on a milk crate in the middle of the desert trying to type reports with the wind whipping her papers around. Every day someone in Media put together a roundup of March events which was read over the phone to local media contacts. A weekly wrapup went to media people all along our route.

The most difficult part of the job was lack of a telephone. Media volunteers had to commandeer a vehicle each day, drive to a pay phone and from there call local newspapers and TV and radio stations, as well as national wire services and other possible sources of publicity. Three-fourths of the job, says Elizabeth, was logistics.

In Rifle, Colorado, Media bought a small bus which functioned as a press office on wheels. The problem of papers and typewriters sliding onto the floor as the driver rounded a curve was never quite solved, but the bus was a more efficient office than the tent. Usually the driver parked near the front gate of camp, so that reporters and important visitors could locate our media headquarters easily.

Mark Nairne, who had worked at the *Hartford Courant*, did advance work for the department, contacting press and broadcast people and setting up interviews in their areas to be held after Marchers arrived. Other department volunteers bought local newspapers, clipped articles about the GPM, organized and photocopied them and made press kits for reporters.

- *CIA*

Most towns and smaller cities, except possibly in Utah, were interested in the March's coming and wanted to have a piece of the action. That meant we had to meet people and explain our mission. Marcher Ann Drissell, who had a gift for designing and putting into effect a complicated organization, was one of several people who volunteered to do outreach. A plan she developed included a department called the Community Interaction Agency, or CIA. (Marchers had a relentless and often ironic sense of humor, which was undoubtedly one of the things that kept us going.) The CIA was to take in and give out information to and from other March departments and the outside world. This plan was accepted, and Ann and peace activist and historian Allen Smith were named national field co-directors. Ann stayed in camp; Allen worked in the field organizing publicity and activities in the largest cities. CIA people who walked with the March handled smaller communities.

The department bought a bus and carpenter Carl Samuelson converted it into an office. (One March joke was that after the March was over people would buy an *office* building and convert it into a bus.)

Stephanie Wald worked at finding out who were the peace activists and organizations in the next state and which churches might help. Towns might have a notion about how they wanted to interface with the March, but often differences had to be settled if what they wanted might not be possible. For instance, a lunchtime rally would not work if the March could not get to the town until midafternoon.

When things went well, CIA might have three or four weeks' lead time for coordinating events; having only a week or less, which also happened, made work difficult.

I will tell my three young daughters that someone cares about their having a place in this world when they grow up.

–Mayor Richard Hatcher of Gary, Indiana, in talk to Marchers

97

As the March went eastward, coordination improved. Publicity about the March made for greater interest in it, and many times local groups, who had not previously worked together, did so to facilitate March events. One woman reported later that she had lived for over 20 years in a community where there were more than a dozen churches that had never worked on anything together. "But when you came, we did. We had to feed you and help you. You brought peace to us."

With the help of Marcher Shabtai Klein, the March got an electronic mailbox message system with equipment that was mostly donated. The Los Angeles March office, as well as field offices and Peace City, then became members of Peacenet, an outfit that provides a nationwide electronic bulletin board and mailboxes. Twice a day, Shabtai would use his computer with modem to phone the Peacenet number. If there were messages in his electronic mailbox, his computer would receive them. He would then print out the messages in the InfoCenter trailer and give them to the appropriate person. In the reverse process, he could send messages via Peacenet to various GPM offices. Having electronic mail capabilities enabled the March to get information often within a day and made communication more efficient.

In Indiana, Carl and Stephanie took over the department and it was they who coordinated the last part of the March.

● *Merchandising*

The idea of selling Great Peace March T-shirts came originally from PRO-Peace, but it seemed like a good one to Sally-Alice Thompson who had been a political activist and teacher in Albuquerque. Sally-Alice ordered some shirts, paid for them herself and was soon making money for our hard-up March. At first her own car was the warehouse for merchandise that included T-shirts, posters, pins, buttons and bumper stickers.

When the department expanded too much for her car, Sally-Alice bought a bus of her own and recruited a group, many of them senior Marchers, to help staff the operation. They set up tables every day at the camp gate, at rallies and at every public event, such as concerts by Collective Vision.

Meantime, Joe Broido, working with the GPM's national office in California, arranged for our branch offices to get supplies of merchandise to sell, sometimes months ahead of the arrival of the March itself.

Sally-Alice and her crew provided much-needed cash from merchandise sales all along the way. But November 15 in Washington was their record—$30,000 in sales in one day.

● *Peace Academy*

From the beginning, education and outreach were an essential mission of the March. That meant we had to have speakers who could talk persuasively about nuclear disarmament in communities along the way.

In Barstow, Craig Dinsdale and other Marchers decided to form an outreach and education department. Craig collected

Two rules of the bookmobile were: Remove your shoes before entering; No sleeping inside

equipment—tape machines, a movie projector and several boxes of supplies—that PRO-Peace had left behind. Then he and Dave Miller set out to buy a bus. In Las Vegas, they found a good one for $4,500, much more than Craig could spend. "Make me an offer I can't refuse," the owner said. Dave explained the March and what the vehicle would be used for.

"How about $1,500?" he asked.

"It's yours," said the owner.

Don Wright, the staunch March supporter who had bought our pumper truck, contributed a black and white TV, a VCR and a generator so that we could show both educational and entertaining tapes. That was the beginning of Peace Academy. Later it acquired a photocopy machine and file cabinets. The Peace Academy bus was one of the best equipped of the March.

Experienced volunteer speakers soon began going out into communities to talk about nuclear issues. Later, Marchers who were interested in learning to speak to groups effectively could attend training sessions which both Peace Academy and outside experts conducted. Paulien Geitenbeek, a Marcher from the Netherlands, was a popular trainer. Her experience conducting street theater among delinquent young people helped her project drama into her sessions. Marchers also flocked to speakers' workshops put on by Joan Bokaer, an educator and well-informed speaker. Through these training sessions—and after actual experience—many Marchers who had never done public speaking before became comfortable and skilled.

As requests for speakers grew, the job of scheduling people to fill engagements became a big one. Speakers had to be matched with audiences and transportation found to and from the event. Some military veterans on the March were good with veterans' groups, and some of the younger Marchers who looked very counterculture did well with some high school students. Sometimes an older and younger speaker would be sent out together.

Often, in smaller towns, someone would come to the March and say, "Can you get a speaker for a radio program that airs in half an hour?" or "I want people to speak to my group and I'll take them there and bring them back. Now!" A Marcher would go to larger cities weeks ahead of the March to set up speaking engagements.

After the first dropping of the bombs on Hiroshima and Nagasaki [August 6 and August 9, 1945] there were no nuclear weapons in the world– they had all been detonated...

In Chicago Marchers spoke in 75 churches and synagogues—all in one day. In New York they were able to fill at least 120 engagements in five days in schools alone, because a month before the rest of us were due to arrive Marcher Adeline McConnell went there and began phoning. Some people recalled that they spent most of their time in New York on the subway going from one engagement to another. Katie McGee spent hours one day handing out subway tokens to 80 Marchers who were going to speak.

No accurate statistics exist to show exactly how many people across the country heard Marchers, but Peace Academy workers "guestimate" that over 100,000 listened to us, and many times that number heard us on radio and TV. And Marchers have continued on the speakers' circuit since the March ended.

Once it became known that Peace Academy needed materials, people both on and off the March donated useful articles and information about nuclear disarmament and peace. Ann Edelman, who had been active in Beyond War, a peace organization, was in charge of literature, which the staff photocopied for distribution. Before our photocopy machine was acquired, duplicating had to be done and paid for. Once Ann and Liane Adams went to a shop with $125 in cash and a stack of articles. They told the March story and asked, "Will you help?" One of the employees said she'd kick in $10 and another offered to contribute something. Then the owner said, "Do all you want."

At the end of the March all the leftover articles were collated and sold in packets to Marchers and friends.

- *Childcare and Schooling*

Concern about childcare and schooling on the March began in Los Angeles where parents spent many hours meeting together. In Barstow they decided they would remain a unit and whenever possible put their tents together in Family Town. Then they moved right into designing caretaking and educational programs for their twenty or so children.

In the original plan, older youngsters—those twelve and up—were to do independent study under the supervision of interested adults. A number of young people did just that. Others kept busy taking care of the littlest children and working at regular

...The nuclear world order began with the Soviet ability [Sept. 19, 1949] to match the United States.

–Christopher Campbell,
Nuclear Weapons
Fact Book

101

March jobs as well as just "hanging out." Some became good speakers in junior and senior high schools.

Parents of the toddlers supervised that group with the help of volunteers, and most little ones managed quite well. They had a huge extended family, and they could roll out of their tents and find a lot of friendly people willing to play with them. A great concern was their physical safety. Watching one of the younger children became a job assignment that many of the adolescents liked. Despite this, and especially for the single parent of a toddler, the caretaking job was very strenuous and required all the support that other parents and the rest of Peace City could provide.

A bus named Kiddie Haul became the toddlers' nursery school. Eventually there was another bus for the kindergarten to fourth grade group, and a third bus for middle school children ages ten and up. All children then had transportation and a place to work and play out of rain and cold. Seats in the first few rows of the busses remained in place and were outfitted with seatbelts. Tables and bookshelves were installed at correct heights and replaced seats at the back.

Adults and children decorated the busses with colorful curtains and pictures. Diane Hara, mother of two young children, had secured donations of children's books and materials before we left Los Angeles. Teachers got additional materials as the March progressed.

For the K-4 group, educator Linda Casassa made a great effort to provide regular schooling—as often as possible—with reading and math in the morning when camp was relatively quiet. In the afternoon, the group went on field trips and it was around these trips that much teaching took place. A year after the March, some parents commented that their children had learned many things about energy, farms and farming, animals and plants, geology and geography and about what happens to some towns when economic conditions change.

Children also were exposed to many intense social interactions, and their teachers made it a point to expose them to peaceful conflict resolution techniques. Midway through the March, Diane Hara overheard a seven-year-old tell an eight-year-old who had hit him, "I don't understand why you are angry with me, but I still want to be your friend and I want to talk with you when you cool down."

I wanted to go on the March because I wanted to grow up, and I might not get a chance if we don't do something about war.

–Crystal Constantine, ten-year-old Marcher

Parents and teachers differed on the need for discipline and structure. Some felt that it was important to build in as much as possible; others objected strenuously. Eventually, all parents accepted the decision that when children were disruptive they would be asked to take time out. Still, some youngsters believed that it was all right to do only what they wanted to do and they were supported in this by some adults.

Another difficulty was the impermanence of life on the March and how children coped with it. Some found it hard to have different

The March was a big stimulus for the youth. I helped the kids organize the Firehouse Youth for Peace and Justice. We mobilized four busses from Iowa to Washington. About 30 high school kids went, and that really began the youth group.

—Ed Fallon, Des Moines

Sam Wolfe demonstrates Peace City efficiency

103

adults working with them each day. Teachers, like other people, worked two days a week and walked the other days. Therefore, children had changing caretakers. Food often looked and tasted strange and it was ready at odd times. Adults and children both reacted to the stresses of the constant moving, to the harsh weather and physical complaints.

But difficulties loom less in memory than the joyful moments of play and adventure. A year after the March, several children remembered their experiences and wrote about them for school assignments. They are very much aware of nuclear and peace issues and know that their parents are among those who work to keep their world safe.

● *Post Office*

Just like any small community, Peace City had a post office. Greg Jones, a Marcher from Montana and former postal employee, set up a system for collecting and delivering mail which operated smoothly for nine months. Anyone who wanted to reach a Marcher addressed the letter in care of General Delivery in the town where the GPM would be five days later. Schedules of post office pickup points were given to Marchers for their families and friends before we left Los Angeles, and the information was always available at Peace City's post office. Letters and packages that arrived after the March had left an area were forwarded to the post office up the line.

The March post office itself had space that Bill Pettijohn let them use in his bus. Volunteers collected March mail from the local post office in the afternoon and took it to camp. There they sorted it alphabetically, and at 5 p.m. people lined up in front of two windows. Those unlucky folks who had no letters were sometimes given a cookie or candy—and once a toothbrush—to make them feel better.

The foregoing is a sample, rather than a complete picture, of how Peace City worked. The department heads and other volunteers mentioned also represent but a fraction of Marchers whose efforts helped us get to Washington.

Chapter V

Diversity, Diversion And Dissent

June 15-16 : North Platte, NE
July 3-6 : Council Bluffs, IA
July 18 : Des Moines, IA
July 31 : Davenport, IA
August 6 : Dixon, IL
August 14-17 : Chicago, IL

From eastern Colorado on, marching was going to be different. In a very real sense a race had begun. Population centers were few, so delays for ceremonies were few, and the number of miles covered each day rose sharply. This would make it possible to keep two special dates. On July 5, in Omaha, Marchers would join the Heartland Peace Pilgrimage which was sponsored by 30 communities of Catholic women religious and several peace groups. Then in Davenport, Iowa, on July 30, we would meet the Mississippi riverboat, *Delta Queen*, which was carrying about 50 Soviet citizens (a cosmonaut, a retired general, some members of the Supreme Soviet, a milkmaid and so on), and about 150 United States citizens, including Admiral Gene LaRocque. An organization,

Promoting Enduring Peace, had assembled this international group, whose participants discussed how to build mutual trust and friendship and shared and compared their lives in between sightseeing trips on shore.

As we made our way across the Midwest we were seeing something at firsthand that was new to most of us: family farms were in a desperate situation. We saw evidence that foreclosures were driving men, women and children off the land. In small towns FOR RENT signs appeared in the windows of many vacant stores, and FOR SALE signs sat in front of farm houses.

Although the Nebraska heat was exhausting and the daily walks were sometimes as long as 25 miles, Marchers were eager to meet the peace-activist nuns and to greet the Soviet-American cruise. We felt a special connection with the Heartland Pilgrimage, because Marcher Buffy Boesen, an energetic nun in the order of Sisters of Loretto, had been closely associated with the nuns who initiated the Heartland walk.

The Heartland Pilgrimage, made up of four columns with eight to a dozen people in each, walked toward Omaha from north, south, east and west. In the Omaha-Council Bluffs area they and the March held joint gatherings. One was an interfaith prayer service in a Council Bluffs high school; another, a gathering and a walk to the headquarters of the Strategic Air Command (SAC) at Offutt Air Force Base.

At SAC headquarters, the nerve center of the United States nuclear forces, the nuns engaged in civil disobedience by crossing into an area forbidden to the public. Those who stepped into outlawed territory were taken away by the military police but were released and given letters forbidding them to engage in similar activity at SAC for one year.

After the protest at the base, Tom Atlee wrote this poem:

> On the asphalt, beyond the white line,
> two rows of
> white, black, female, male, young
>   (mostly neat in camouflage fatigues)
> guards watch, noticing, listening,
> thinking, experiencing the strangely

While we were marching, June 14: Fifty thousand march for peace in Winnepeg, Manitoba.

deep event we make as
we cross the line
reciting dedication, truth or song
one by one
lead us away
as one by one
the tears come—
"Real men don't drop bombs"
the T-shirts say. And to our camp
one by one they later come
Defenses fall with the tears
one
by
one
For peace is everyone's
profession.

As individuals, many Marchers joined this CD (civil disobedience) action at SAC, but the March as a whole, here and everywhere else, did not actually sponsor acts of civil disobedience. In doing so, the March honored the wishes of many who wanted to act within the law—as well as honoring pledges made to donors who had been told that all March actions would be legal. The control that these donors exercised over policy was very real in this regard, and it raised questions more easily asked than answered. Was the policy of engaging in legal actions only, which was purchased in a sense by much-needed contributions, better for the cause of nuclear disarmament than massive civil disobedience would have been? And would the March have been able to proceed at all without this money?

The civil disobedience action at SAC headquarters and the rendezvous with the Heartland Pilgrimage were part of ongoing relations with religious groups that had been important in many different ways from the very beginning. Less than a month out of Barstow, and with overwhelming problems ahead of them, the Marchers had paused in the desert north of St. George, Utah, to celebrate Passover. Jew and non-Jew alike sat in the sand eating gefilte fish, haroset, turkey and tzimmes while Rabbi Mel Hecht of Las Vegas, with the help of Jewish Marchers, read the traditional words of the Seder.

It was tempting to pack up and go along. Everyone was so kind. I thought, "What can I do to help?" I couldn't afford to do much, but I took some food out to camp.

–Patty Guthrie, owner, Patty's Pantry, Kearney, NE

Joe Broido had enlisted the aid of Marchers Gerda Lawrence, Shelah Notkoff and Tom Krieg, a Korean student, to prepare the dinner and transport it from Los Angeles and Las Vegas to the campsite in Utah. The symbolism of both the desert setting and the recent release of the March from Barstow, and the parallels with ancient Jewish history, were not lost on the assembled travelers.

The Passover celebration was the only all-March sectarian service during the eight-and-one-half-month journey, but several ecumenical services were held, to which all Marchers and local citizens were invited. Although many religious leaders had called the nuclear arms race the most important moral issue of our time, religious communities along the route of the March, as well as in the rest of the country, appeared deeply divided over how to respond to it. This division was reflected in the different reactions that the GPM generated in churches along the route.

For example, religious groups provided camping space (indoor sleeping space in bad weather), thousands of hot meals, financial and moral support, a public forum from which Marchers spoke, a clearinghouse and hosts for the Marcher-in-the-Home program, religious services for Marchers and countless kindnesses. Probably the GPM could not have survived the eight-and-one-half months without that support. It was the churches in Claremont, California, that came to the rescue the third day of the trek, and the last campsite in Washington was on the grounds of St. Paul's Theological College.

But there were also opposition and indifference. Most Mormons in Utah, although not visibly hostile, kept their distance. In Grand Island, Nebraska, Margaret Heim, a woman in her 70s and a member of the First Christian Church, contacted members of several churches about participating in the potluck that was being held for the March. "I got lots of no's," she said. "I had lined up several women from the Catholic Church to bring food. One of them called me back to say their priest wouldn't let them participate. But enough good Christians did respond and we had ample food to serve the potluck."

Later, in Carlisle, Pennsylvania, members of the Plainfield Faith Baptist Church met the March carrying signs reading, "Don't Forget to Stop in Moscow" and "Don't Disarm America, Rearm It."

Often it was the priest or minister who supported the March and its goals, even though he encountered resistance from parishoners. Dewey Sands, pastor of the Elim Covenant Church in Moline, Illinois, described his dilemma: "I was very responsive and supportive because the March spoke to concerns very important to me. I struggled how to best communicate that concern to my congregation....I guess I don't always have the guts to say what I feel." Rev. Sands invited six or eight people from the March to come to his midweek Bible study group. "In our Christian context we think about the sacrifices of missionaries who give up their lives to go to another country to spread the gospel. One of the Marchers who came to the Bible study, although he called himself an atheist or agnostic (I forget which) had that same kind of commitment."

Many individuals were participating in the March out of a religious conviction that nuclear weapons are immoral. They approached peace in ways sought by followers of Gandhi or Buddha or Ram Dass or the New Age or pacifist leaders in the Jewish and Christian faiths. All-inclusive concepts of love and humanity moved people of all ages to march—and helped keep them marching. This same emphasis on humanity attracted people who had little or no religious motivation. Believers and non-believers walked and worked together, and usually neither made it a condition of cooperation that all have a common view on matters theological. Believers in the healing powers of crystals or the efficacy of prayer walked side by side with total skeptics. All knew that the world had to avoid nuclear war if they were to go on believing or disbelieving.

The compelling importance of a nuclear-free world produced a very broad kind of coalition that demonstrated, as few other things could, how widespread was the rejection of nuclear weapons.

There were two Roman Catholic nuns (from different orders), several Protestant ministers, children of ministers, a number of Methodists, Presbyterians, Lutherans, Unitarians, Quakers, Jews, a woman Episcopal Deacon, Mennonites, several Buddhist monks, some agnostics and atheists. There were also New Agers, numerologists, astrologers, Native American animists, Jungian and Freudian analysts, mystics, sceptics, computer analysts, Democrats, Anarchists, Republicans, several Communist sympathizers, auto mechanics, metalworkers, retired professors, carpenters, members of Alcoholics Anonymous, lesbians, gays, Vietnam veterans, no doubt one or more FBI or CIA agents, teachers, a few Blacks and

I got a feeling of hope for the first time in maybe 20 years that people were going to make a difference, and that maybe somewhere I can fit in this process.

–Wind Usedan, March supporter

109

Hispanics, students, many musicians, one clown, several lawyers, a vitamin salesperson, a professional gambler—and on and on.

Probably no other American community the size of Peace City could boast more diversity, and certainly few communities have been challenged to hold themselves together while experiencing the stress of moving almost every day from one place to another.

Marchers came from all 50 states and 10 foreign countries. Mark Huffman, a reporter for *The Vail Trail* in Vail, Colorado, commented, "The day I was there, a woman from Texas, a grandmother, was serving food, and right next to her was a young woman dressed like she was from Nepal. She'd changed her name to some single name, something different. It was quite a zoo."

Marcher Florence Douthit agreed. She wrote in the *Oakland Tribune*: "What the hundreds of Marchers have experienced in some ways has been like an old-fashioned revival meeting, a Boy Scout jamboree, a university seminar, a low-budget soap opera, a supercharged encounter session, a five-ring circus, a nature expedition, and a solemn crusade to rattle the world's consciousness and awaken a sense of indignation."

The surprising fact that such a diverse group could live together peacefully was not lost on spectators along the way. Even so, some Marchers worried—and much discussion went on among them—about the strange costumes and hairstyles adopted by a few participants. Anne Macfarlane of New Zealand was one who worried. At one point in Nebraska, there was a semi-serious "dress rebellion." Ann remembers that day in her book, *Feet Across America*: "The worst day of the March for me was when young men started to appear, wearing frocks. Some days before, one or two of the seniors had spoken with concern about the dirty, torn and bizarre clothing of some of the younger men. This had provoked the rebellion. 'If the seniors want a dress code, we'll give them a dress code,' they said. Tonight was the dress rehearsal for the way they intended to march tomorrow. Their civil rights were at stake. They were entitled to wear anything they chose.

"I began to despair. The police had already been called to the camp because a child was wandering around naked. 'This is the Bible Belt you are in,' he told us. We knew people were apprehensive about us and now some of our men were going to

> *What a waste it would be after four billion tortuous years of evolution if the dominant organism contrived its own self-destruction.*
>
> *–Carl Sagan*

march in frocks. I began to feel as though all my efforts were being negated by those who were making us look foolish with their insistence on their right to wear dresses.

"Some of the seniors dialogued with them, pointing out that the nuclear disarmament message was nullified by their behavior, the conservative nature of the area we were in, and thank goodness some of the men responded by agreeing to dress normally. I didn't have the heart to debate it."

Nevertheless, our varied outward appearance did signal diversity, and often it was viewed positively. Recalling the March as it made its way through Kearney, Nebraska, Nancy Taylor, a reporter for the *Kearney Daily Hub*, said, "They were common people of all ages. They didn't hold to a stereotype, although a stereotype preceded the March. Anyone who made an effort to be with the March changed their mind about the stereotype."

In November, Marchers and students attended an event at Johns Hopkins University. Afterward, Gretchen Van Utt, the university's chaplain and an organizer for the event, commented that the students there were "very moved by the diversity. They couldn't categorize them [the Marchers], because they were so diverse. That was good."

A reporter for the Long Island, New York, *Newsday* wrote: "A handful of holy men and individualists make up the vanguard. Some are eccentric, a circumstance that emphasizes the openness of the Great Peace March to cultural and ideological diversity, so long as nuclear disarmament has its place near the heart."

The rich diversity of the March community, while demonstrating the broad range of society that was speaking out against nuclear arms, made it difficult to reach agreement on many other things. The Marcher contract, which a majority had been willing to sign when we were in the Mojave Desert, continued to be an area of disagreement.

This contract was a document establishing a standard of conduct to which most Marchers could subscribe—no alcohol or drugs in camp, no engaging in acts of violence, participation in work, abiding by any regulations that the duly-established March officials felt necessary to draw up.

Some Marchers believed that the contract would settle much of the dissension by spelling out what the community agreed on and what common sense required as a way of holding the March together. How wrong that belief was!

At any rate, the Board had decided in Denver on June 1 to try to bring about calm by holding yet another election. Perhaps the active anti-leadership group would be persuaded by a new Board to cooperate in the solution to very real problems, such as drugs, alcohol and rejection of the Board decisions. But far from spreading oil on the waters, the new election stirred up new waves. Anti- and pro-contract groups formed, and 45 candidates ran for election to the Board.

Candidates issued statements—platforms of a sort. John Records said in his announcement, "I don't see the issue as being the signing of the contract so much as the community's need to have an agreed-upon, enforceable standard of conduct....We could do this without having every single person sign the contract." And so, John concluded, "I offer reconciliation of differing views; I have a lot of practice in finding a middle ground in working out compromises."

Two other candidates, on the other hand, Peter Megginson and Mary Giardina, who were part of the group who set up tents around a black flag, made a joint statement which declared: "Decision making and departmental supervision are functions that belong not with the Board, but with the March Community." They also proposed to involve in decision making "those working across the country for the March." Just how these scattered individuals across the country could take part in quick decisions often needed by the ever-moving March was not clear.

Mary and Peter also urged that all decisions about finances be made by the entire community. It was their contention that ideally the Board's financial role should be limited to raising funds the March would need. But how could the Board guarantee contributors that all March activities would be legal if it then surrendered the funds to people over whom it had no control and who might well spend it in support of such illegal activities as civil disobedience?

On June 16 in Grand Island, Nebraska, all the Board members (Allan Affeldt, Coleen Ashly, Tim Carpenter, Dan Chavez, Evan

Conroy, Franklin Folsom and Judith Rane) resigned and an election took place. Forty-five people received votes for the seven positions, and the results were inconclusive. In a run-off the following were elected: Coleen Ashly, Dan Chavez, Evan Conroy, Franklin Folsom, Mary Giardina, Peter Megginson and John Records.

Since the election placed on the Board at least two members who were committed to stripping the Board of all effective power, and since two other Board members often seemed to share that view, there remained only peer pressure as a way of obtaining compliance with rulings. And the peers were so deeply divided that they could not exert pressure in a common direction.

It was becoming clear that the Board, the City Council, the Entrance-Exit Committee and the Judicial Board had no effective way of enforcing their decisions. Betty Phelps described the situation after attending a Judicial Board hearing that dealt with drug and alcohol use in camp: "Three lashes with a wet noodle is not the sort of remedy that will rehabilitate the hard-core subculture that we have rebelling against our rules."

The March continued to manifest internal disunity, and consequently in the view of some Marchers, to lose effectiveness.

Board of Directors meeting in Lincoln, Nebraska

What the March could have been like if all participants had bound themselves by an agreement will never be known. All we can do is note that earlier marches that had strong central leadership, such as the Hunger Marches of the Great Depression and Martin Luther King Jr.'s Poor People's March a generation later, did have significant results. Perhaps our March would have been stronger and more effective if the simple standards of the March contract had been enforced. Those who opposed it would have been separated from the March and encouraged to find another way of working for peace.

Board of Directors meeting in the shower room at Edgewater Park, Cleveland, OH

On the other hand, some feared, to have lopped off a segment of the March body could well have proved fatal. Despite the internal divisions, we arrived in Washington on time, and along the way we talked with thousands of Americans who were largely unaware of our internal strife but did hear our common message.

In spite of the chaos, the Board of Directors, secure under the law, continued to try to give the best direction it could. And the March continued to move forward day after day. Essential departments functioned: sites were secured, vehicles got fixed, food was bought and prepared, and life went on.

At the same time, ferment continued right up to November 15. Whether this ferment was in some part manipulated by forces external to the March, as some suspected, may never be known, but one thing was clear: many of the Marchers were spirited rebels who had set out to get the strongest of governments to destroy thousands of the deadliest weapons ever invented. If these folks could take on the governments of the United States and, as some would have it, of the USSR, they could certainly rise up in opposition to a handful of fellow Marchers who, as members of the Board of Directors, were the nearest visible authority.

Disagreements were not limited to matters of basic policy. They covered a whole range of questions, some quite unlikely. Should the March buy a horse and wagon to attract attention at the head of the line? If so, what could be done with the manure? (Someone did buy a large farm wagon and helpers pulled it by hand a long way.)

Pete Seeger, who joined us on several occasions, commented on the fact that the March stayed together, "when every tenet of logic dictated that it should have broken up. The disagreements over lifestyle were as strong as any group of human beings could have. But they agreed, 'We will arrive in D.C. at the same time, come hell or high water.' It shows how people can put aside great differences and form a consensus if they have common goals."

An ongoing campaign for more grassroots or consensual control versus leadership by elected representatives had absorbed a good deal of energy, especially in the first months of the March. The push for a consensual form of decision-making came from a group that felt the incorporation in California had happened without the consent of the Marchers. The Board of Directors, they said, was

On nuclear arms issues, paranoia about the Soviet Union has so paralyzed American policy that we have rejected some of the most historic peace overtures of the nuclear age.

*–David Cortright,
Co-Director,
SANE/FREEZE*

115

similar in structure to PRO-Peace and there was a fear that decisions would be made by a few at the top.

To some, the achievement of complete community democracy began to be the prime objective of the March. At times it appeared that they were forgetting the original goal—education and action to obtain nuclear disarmament. But generally speaking, the complaints were not so much that the governing bodies were making the wrong decisions—just that the decisions were being made the wrong way.

The keen interest of Marchers in the structure of the decision-making process attested to the vitality and involvement of the group. One of the strengths of the GPM was the ability we had to disagree and, whether the issue was resolved or not, continue down the road together.

The GPM was the kind of mass of humanity with which Walt Whitman would have felt at home. There was room in his largeness of spirit for all this great variety, but the good gray poet would not have felt comfortable with some of the small-spirited bickering he would have found among people who had such a great purpose. In the fertile soil of the March, the idealistic notions of complete democracy as well as of rank-and-file unanimity easily took root. One device that was aimed at achieving unanimity was the practice of forming "crystal circles" or "talking stick" circles. Let one of the March publications, *The Weekly Peace* describe it:

> Inspired by the American Indians who use a "talking stick" to facilitate their meetings, a crystal circle is a group of 3-20 people (more or less) who leave behind combativeness and ego-tripping to build a great truth together. At the start, they set their crystal, talking stick, stone or other aesthetic, agreed-upon object in the middle of the circle and—in silence or guided imagery—take a moment to grant it the power (or right) to guide them towards greater group truth.

The stick or crystal is then picked up in turn by those who wish to speak and held as they are speaking. The system reduced frustration, shouting and chaos, but not all Marchers were happy with the implication that they might not be telling the truth without the presence of a crystal or that the crystal had some kind of supernatural power.

Another issue, which was less often articulated but lay behind some of the conflicts, was a philosophical disagreement on how best to reach our goal of global nuclear disarmament. A sizeable group of Marchers felt that nuclear weapons are but a symptom of society's ills and that peace can only be achieved by each individual searching for and finding inner peace and exemplifying that in his or her daily life. The other faction believed just as strongly that all our political and social forces need to be marshalled against the common threat and that efforts in a different direction are harmful.

All in all, the March demonstrated that a portion of individualistic, generally middleclass, non-political America was in motion against nuclear weapons. Looking at the March, right-wingers could not say—and be believed—that peace activism was limited to the Left.

Although wholehearted support for the March was lacking in Nebraska, Midwest hospitality was evident. The advance team was given unexpected cooperation by farmers who okayed our camping on their land. Local churches and chapters of Nebraskans for Peace put on potluck dinners. Farm families occasionally greeted us with cold drinks or an invitation to rest on the front lawn or cool off under the garden hose. In one rural area a teenage boy roared off through the cornfields on his motorcycle to return with a quart of soda which he gave to a hot and thirsty Marcher.

Before we reached Lincoln, the Women's Collective, an active support group within the March community, had made arrangements with the Lincoln YWCA for a weekend of hospitality. The Y provided a potluck dinner, showers and sleeping space on the gymnasium floor for 150 women and children. They were only too happy to be inside during a thunderstorm that dumped four inches of rain on the rest of us camped outside in Peace City.

In Iowa we received a hearty welcome from members of Iowa peace organizations as we crossed the Missouri River on July 3. Before reaching camp, we fell in step behind an energetic Omaha parade group, Cookie's Pride Drill Team, who walked into Iowa with us. This all-Black group danced and drummed in the heat, dressed in their magenta tails, white pants and silver top hats. We followed in our mismatched, sweaty walking garb.

The president of Grinnell College let us put up our tents on the

Marchers calling themselves Test Ban Affinity Group, or T-BAG, report that they have got 800 letters sent to Senators and Representatives asking them to cut funding for nuclear weapons tests.
–Peace City News, Nov. 7, 1986

117

campus. Farmers along the way east kept us supplied with vegetables. We even had sweet corn for breakfast. And once we passed a farm where head lettuce growing in a field spelled out PEACE.

The GPM field offices in Des Moines and Iowa City had been planning for our arrival ever since PRO-Peace days. Their efforts culminated in a very successful Marcher-in-the-Home program in Des Moines and an extensive program of speakers in churches in Iowa City. A woman in the Iowa City water department put the GPM schedule in with all the water bills she sent out before we arrived.

When the March reached Davenport, Iowa, on July 30, the crowd assembled on the banks of the Mississippi looked more like a huge family gathering than a meeting between cold-war enemies. Citizens of the Quad-Cities (Davenport and Bettendorf, Iowa, and Moline and Rock Island, Illinois) and 500 Marchers embraced, sang and exchanged gifts and addresses with a contingent of Soviet people and Americans who were traveling from St. Paul, Minnesota, to St. Louis on the *Delta Queen.* One of the 46 Soviets on the cruise, Cosmonaut Gregory Grechko, spoke briefly, saying, "My English is very bad. I think my heart says it better than my tongue. I like you, my American friends."

Soviet citizens and Americans exchange peace signs as the Delta Queen docks in Davenport, Iowa.

Peace City ceremonial mayor Diane Clark noted the irony of calling the Mississippi "ours," for the waters of the great river flow out into the oceans and around the planet. "Are we not all one planet?" she asked the cheering crowd. The emotional meeting ended with Marchers and local people standing shoulder to shoulder singing "All we are saying is give peace a chance!" as the riverboat shoved off from the dock.

Less than a week later, on August 6, Hiroshima Day, we gathered on the steps of the courthouse in Dixon, Illinois, where Ronald Reagan had once lived. While Rev. Thomas Shepard read a graphic description of what had happened in Hiroshima in 1945, church bells began to toll and the speaker stopped in mid-sentence. Marchers "froze" in place as if fried by a nuclear explosion, and long, silent seconds passed. After two minutes, Rev. Shepard continued, "As the bells rang, what had been important suddenly became unimportant. We are reminded how fragile we are." Later that day, in a Keys-and-Trees ceremony, we presented a peace tree to city officials to be planted in the garden of Reagan's boyhood home.

August 14: Marchers climbed out of their sleeping bags at 3 a.m. This wasn't easy, but the excitement of knowing that we would be walking into downtown Chicago in a few hours helped nudge sleepy people from their tents. The early departure was necessary because of a rally and welcome by Mayor Harold Washington in the Windy City.

When predominantly white Marchers trooped through Black neighborhoods on the outskirts of Chicago later that morning, they were greeted by smiles, shouts and honking horns as well as quizzical looks. People leaned out of windows in their dilapidated tenements to wave. As two neighborhood boys fell in line with the March, the younger asked the older one, "Does this mean there won't be no more wars?" A work-weary woman poked her head out of the door of a rundown restaurant and exclaimed to herself, "They're all white!" All white or not, the GPM got a very warm welcome from the Black community of Chicago.

The police had blocked off Michigan Avenue in the Loop for the parade through downtown, but it was a parade largely ignored by the hurrying lunch time crowd of junior executives and office workers. They seemed more annoyed than inspired by the banner-

The impact of the March was very substantial here. A good portion of that was the meeting between the Peace Cruise and the March.

–Thomas Hart, Mayor of Davenport, IA

119

carrying, enthusiastic invaders. At Buckingham Fountain in Grant Park on the shore of Lake Michigan, a few hundred supporters and some local politicians greeted the Marchers who were a bit sobered by the indifferent reception they had just received in the Loop. Spirits lifted when Mayor Washington reminded listeners that Chicago was a nuclear-free zone—the largest in the United States—and proclaimed the following Sunday "Survival Sunday" in honor of the March.* Meantime, Casey Kasem, disc jockey for the radio show, "America's Top 40," was doing a radio fund-raiser for the GPM. A twelve-hour appeal brought in $2,200.

During their four-day stay, the Marchers camped in North Chicago, far removed from downtown. A request to camp in Grant Park, the scene of the 1968 violence during the Democratic Convention, had been turned down by the Chicago Park District. Camping space in North Park Village next to the Bohemian Cemetery was provided just hours before the March entered the city. An open house at camp the first night drew a small crowd of people who poked around, listened to speakers and for $5 ate March food, standing up, just like everyone else.

Marchers spoke at 75 Chicago-area churches on Sunday morning. That evening in Willamette a good-sized crowd attended an interfaith service at the Baha'i Temple where the Hiroshima Peace Flame was shared with the Baha'i congregation.

In Chicago, Judith Rane organized the "Shadow Project" to commemorate Hiroshima Day—the day when the atomic bomb vaporized people but left shadows imprinted on sidewalks and streets. Judith began by asking a number of Marchers to pose in bright light beside a big sheet of white plastic stretched on the ground. Then she outlined with marking pen the long shadows they cast on the plastic, scissored out the figures and so had a group of silhouettes of people in various poses.

Later, riding through Chicago streets, Judith spotted a wooden wall around a construction site and got permission to use it for

The March engaged children imaginatively. It was an event that was understandable to them.

–Adrienne Hurvitz, Chicago Peace Museum

---

* What is a nuclear-free zone? Here is Section 202.2 of the Chicago Municipal Code: "No person shall knowingly, within the City of Chicago, design, produce, deploy, launch, maintain or store nuclear weapons or components of nuclear weapons." At the time of the GPM there were 108 nuclear-free zones in the United States. Chicago joined the list on March 12, 1986. New Zealand is a nuclear-free country. "Creating a nuclear-free zone [in Europe] would undercut NATO's military strategy to defend Europe. NATO has refused to rule out using nuclear weapons first in response to a Soviet conventional attack."–Charles Redman, State Department spokesperson, *New York Times*, January 6, 1988

The shadows on our gear trailer are a reminder that after the Hiroshima bombing all that remained of some vaporized victims were their shadows on the sidewalk.

shadow pictures. She and some helpers tacked up the plastic silhouettes on the gray wall and splashed whitewash around the edges of them. When the plastic was taken down, gray shadows appeared, outlined in white.

Unfortunately, this very impressive reminder of nuclear holocaust remained on the wall only a few days before the construction company, through a misunderstanding, had it painted over. But Marchers remembered the effectiveness of the shadows, and before long a new set, outlined in black, appeared on the sides of one of our trailers, reflecting this time not death but life in camp.

The big Chicago event set up by the advance team to spread the March message took place Sunday in Lincoln Park along the shore of Lake Michigan. The timing and the setting seemed ideal for attracting a large crowd, and about 5,000 made their way around the six stations or booths set up to provide information and displays about March life and the arms race. A rally, part of the Lincoln Park event, drew a few hundred to hear Betty Thomas of *Hill Street Blues* and Studs Terkel, author and radio personality. Terkel told listeners, "American society has to make up its mind if it has a life wish or a death wish."

It does not take a majority of people to bring about change.
—Frances Kissling, President, Catholics for a Free Choice

Peace City in western Illinois

Attracting almost as much media attention as the Survival Sunday event was the confrontation of a long-haired Marcher father and his conservatively-dressed, counter-demonstrating son. The father, Jim Wiggins, was master of ceremonies for the rally. His son, Joe Wiegand, with about 50 College Republicans carrying placards, demonstrated against the GPM event. The family war about peace ended with father and son agreeing to disagree.

The days in Chicago were not unproductive, but once again Marchers had learned that large cities, for the most part, were not the places where they could expect large crowds and consistent support. As Kathleen Hendrix of the *Los Angeles Times* wrote after the March left Chicago, "Granting the reality of the march as it has developed, and the time and place it is happening in, many are beginning to suggest that it may be that the individual contacts—the message of hope that individuals can make a difference by getting involved, writing their lawmakers—are the march's greatest strengths." The dramatic visions of David Mixner were finally fading, but in their place something more practical—and more profound—was beginning to emerge.

Chapter VI

Gathering Momentum

August 19 : Gary, IN
August 27 : Shipshewana, IN
September 12-14 : Cleveland, OH
September 19-20 : Youngstown, OH
September 25-26 : Pittsburgh, PA
October 8 : Carlisle, PA

After we left Chicago and entered Gary, Indiana, we encountered the first of many depressed industrial areas through which the March was to pass. The schedule called for a stop at the mammoth U.S. Steel plant which had once provided jobs for over 30,000 steelworkers. Only 5,000 worked there now.

Support of the March by organized labor had not been strong, and Marchers hoped to increase interest here by passing out information about the link between the arms race and the decline of jobs in industry. We joined pickets in a rally at the plant, where Mayor

Richard Hatcher said, "Peace is a complex of many issues. Those who care for peace enough to walk across the country in support of it must also be for racial equality, women's rights and job opportunities for the young."

From Gary, the March moved into rural Indiana where we shared country roads with the horse-drawn black buggies of Amish farmers and their families. "The only movement slower than their horses," said Marcher Ralph Vrana, "was our March."

At Shipshewana, camp for the night was on the grounds of an elementary school in a large Amish settlement. The two groups found that, in spite of their many outward differences, there were several common bonds between them. The Amish, a religious community originally from Germany, live a simple life. They have clung to their old ways, and many of them disdain modern conveniences such as automobiles and electricity. They are strong believers in nonviolence, and the men have traditionally received conscientious objector status when called for military service.

"We had barely set up our tents," Ralph said, "when wave after wave of school children descended on us, with their teachers. They wanted to know everything about us." Ralph, himself a former teacher, had lost his job because he opposed the Diablo Canyon Nuclear Plant which he thought unsafe.

Women and little girls in black bonnets, men and boys in black hats, wearing pants held up by suspenders—all shared a potluck supper with other local people and Marchers.

Arlene Lazzaro, the second grade teacher and president of the Town Board, had her class meet the March children during the day, and at night she took part in the Keys-and-Trees ceremony. Afterward she said, "This community is very peaceful. They all understood why you were walking. Teachers here all thought it was a good experience for the children. It was good for the town, too. It's so sheltered."

Following along the shore of Lake Michigan and Lake Erie in Indiana and Ohio, Marchers enjoyed good weather and friendly folks. It was a pleasure to walk. A special boost to spirits was a contingent from peace organizations in Michigan. About 200 supporters drove to Ohio and walked with the March for a day.

Alexa Nadeau, the youngest Marcher

If there was a nuclear war, I would miss myself.

—A child

The GPM had covered more than two-thirds of the way to Washington, and most people felt sure nothing could stop them now. In this upbeat mood everyone (with the exception of some Spirit Walkers) rode the ferry *Goodtime I* across Sandusky Bay in Ohio. Otherwise our route would have required crossing a bridge over the bay where pedestrians were not permitted. When the advance people had inquired about the *Goodtime I*, owner Herb Fryan of Cleveland offered its use at no charge, and the crew, including Captain Dennis Wieber and organist Mickey Chambers, donated their time. On the hour-and-a-half ride, some Marchers danced on the decks to old tunes hammered out by Mickey Chambers, while others enjoyed food and drink from the snack bar or just sat and watched the seagulls fly by.

Between Toledo and Cleveland, on the shore of Lake Erie, sits Davis Bessie nuclear power plant. The March route took us down the highway bordering the facility, and we were to camp on power plant property. When Marchers found out about this unfortunate choice, almost everyone agreed that the site was unacceptable. How could a group opposing nuclear weapons sleep on the grounds of a plant that was producing material used in those weapons? But there was no other possible site within miles. The problem was finally solved by giving us two options: we could pass Davis Bessie and walk to our next site at Bergman's Orchards—a distance of 32 miles; or we could walk to the power plant, shuttle in cars and busses to Bergman's, then return in vehicles to the pickup point the next day and walk on from there. Supporters from Toledo came out to help with the shuttling, but many Marchers walked the entire distance in one day.

In Cleveland, something new and significant happened. A stable committee, dating back to PRO-Peace days, had been at work preparing for the arrival of the March on September 13, a date that would coincide with the annual Walkathon organized by Greater Cleveland Freeze. In 1985, 600 Clevelanders had taken part. This year the Freeze organizers hoped to double that figure, but they had not calculated on the enthusiasm the March would stir up. Instead of the hoped for 1,200, over 5,000 Clevelanders turned out and paid for the privilege of walking with the Great Peace March.

The support of unions was visible during the Walkathon, as it had been in the preceding days when the March passed through distressed steel manufacturing centers in Illinois and Indiana. In addi-

People here are tired of meetings. Being able to walk with the March invited people to participate in a different way.

–Diane Brown, Chair of YWCA Peace Coalition, Toledo, OH

125

tion, the Left showed the first signs of giving active support to the March. Earlier, the publications and parties of the Left had looked at glitzy PRO-Peace with skepticism, and they paid little attention to the reorganized Great Peace March. But the GPM had showed such remarkable vitality and persistence that in Cleveland part of the Left press began to take notice. A reporter for the *People's Daily World* was on hand and someone from the paper would accompany the March for much of the next two months. In the Walkathon, a contingent from the Communist Party walked under its banner. Some Marchers were concerned about the addition of the Communist Party to the loose coalition supporting the March, but the GPM's spirit of tolerance and inclusiveness prevailed.

Until now, correspondents for the Soviet media had not paid great attention to the March, but in Cleveland a *Tass* correspondent followed events closely, and from then on eastward, Soviet reporters and photographers made frequent appearances. Their country was coming to regard the March as a significant development in the campaign against nuclear weapons. This became very evident after the March ended, and the Soviet Peace Committee agreed to permit a joint Soviet-American citizens' walk from Leningrad to Moscow.

The Cleveland gathering also attracted interest much closer to home. Ohio's governor, Richard Celeste, spoke to Marchers and Walkathoners before they started their procession through the city. After noting with approval that there were 250 active peace organizations in Ohio, Celeste said of the nuclear arms race, "It only makes us less secure each day, each week, each month it goes on." And he added that he opposed Star Wars and supported peace studies in the curricula of Ohio's colleges.

Representative Louis Stokes called for a one year moratorium on US testing of nuclear weapons, for reduced spending on Star Wars and for US compliance with the SALT II Treaty. Another public official, US Senator Howard Metzenbaum, visited our camp at Edgewater Park and spoke to us using our bullhorn.

Such official support and the friendly presence of the Walkathoners raised Marchers' spirits, and equally important, Cleveland sent them off with a substantial contribution of badly needed dollars. Even the police contributed enthusiasm—again and again they sounded their sirens and horns to call attention to the peaceful throng.

After I got to talking with the Marchers...I sat up there [at camp] the whole day. It kinda got to me. It's my generation that's going to have to deal with the problem. We've got to do something about it.
—Robbie Knuth, high school student

It was mid-September now, and schools were back in session. On the way eastward, in Girard, Ohio, Marchers were greeted by the ringing of church bells and by rows of school children out on the sidewalk to meet them. St. Mary's Catholic School welcomed us for lunch, and the pupils thronged around their guests asking questions and displaying their drawings and signs about wars, weapons and peace. School principal Sister Mary Alyce said a year later, "To have the kids participate was an experience they'll never forget. It was one of the highlights of the year."

When Marchers talked and listened in schools, they came more and more to agree with Dr. John Mack, professor of psychiatry at Harvard Medical School, who has said, "The threat of nuclear annihilation has penetrated deeply into young people's consciousness." Children, Marchers discovered, are angry at adults for creating a scary world, but seldom have a chance to observe that some grownups are working to eliminate the threat they feel. Thousands of children along the route of the GPM met or heard such grownups.

Dale Malleck, a 70 year-old retired metalworker from Denver, often talked to students about how important peace is to them. "I tried to make them realize it's their life that's in jeopardy." Recalling one meeting with a group of junior high students, he says, "I had just written to the President the day before, and I asked the class if they'd like to hear my letter. One little girl said she'd like to hear it, and almost before I'd finished reading it another girl said,

March children studying in their bus-classroom

127

I used to feel that I didn't want to bring another child into the world with all the uncertainty. After our contact with the March I changed my mind.

—Myrta Brown-Velez, who had a child a year after seeing the March

'I'll write.' Then the teacher jumped in and said she'd give an A to anyone who wrote a letter and showed it to her. That got 'em going."

In a high school class, Bob Alei, 29, an electrical engineer and a City Manager in Peace City, got an alert response when he brought out a container of BBs. To illustrate the size of the superpower arsenal of nuclear weapons, Bob asked the students to close their eyes. Then he began to drop BBs, one at a time, into a metal bucket. Each one, he explained, represented one megaton—a million tons—of TNT. Three BBs represented all the firepower of all Allied weapons used in World War II—three megatons. How much firepower is there in the world today? Bob slowly poured into the bucket a steady stream of BBs. The little balls clanged on and on and on—19,000 of them. Then silence. "It scared me," one student finally said. "I started to think about all kinds of things."

Others "found lots to talk about later," their teacher said. "They paid attention." This very effective demonstration, originated by Beyond War, startled many audiences all across the country in churches, civic organizations, peace groups, schools and finally in front of the Lincoln Memorial in Washington on November 15.

Marcher Lynn McGee found that elementary school children often got to the heart of the matter. "I asked a second grade class what they could do for peace, and one small student said, 'We could love everyone more.'"

Kids had a connection to the March in many ways. At a New Year's party in 1986, the guests all wrote on slips of paper the things they wanted to give up in the coming year and threw the slips onto the burning logs in the fireplace. Unexpectedly, children who had been upstairs joined the adults with slips of their own to burn. They had all drawn bombs and missiles which they wanted to get out of their lives in the year ahead. The 14-year-old baby sitter who accompanied the youngsters, told everyone that for as long as she could remember she had been afraid she would not live to grow up. A few days later, civil rights activists Cathy and Dick Wherley, who had been at the party, saw a news story about the March and decided to join. "The kids got the ball rolling," Cathy said later.

There were over 60 children on the March at one time or another, and they had an important effect on the people who saw them. As John Records, father of two young girls, said, "The role of children

was important in opening hearts of people along the way. It gave them access to the March which they might not otherwise have found." The older March kids were often asked to visit classrooms in towns along the route. The visits from young people who were actually participating in a peace action gave school children a chance to meet others their age with whom they could identify.

The children of Peace City didn't just visit schools; they attended their own, even in the summer when other kids were on vacation. By and large, March children enjoyed their school. Brent Hier, 15, of Boulder, Colorado, said of his experience, "On the March you could learn whatever you wanted from the people there. One night someone told me all about Japanese history. You got so much more than you could ever get at [regular] school."

There were, of course, times when children, like adults, found adjusting to a mobile life difficult. Coleen Ashly overheard her six-year-old daughter say: "Do we *have* to go to a children's museum again?" The first few weeks on the March were hardest for Dwarka Bonner's three-and-a-half-year-old son, Hari. There were no small toilet seats for the young children, and Hari was scared of the porta-potties. But before long he followed the older kids and his problems disappeared.

After the March, Mirah seemed much more grown up. [She was 12 at the time.] She was used to being treated as a responsible person.

—Jay Zeitlyn, father of Mirah, a Marcher

129

Daniel, Katie McGee's nine-year-old son, became very tired of traveling. However, he settled down once he returned home and began to catch up academically on what he missed during the March.

Often kids were given special treatment. Communities repeatedly provided treats. They opened public swimming pools (which sometimes resulted in all Marchers getting free showers), and an amusement park near Kent, Ohio, gave them free rides. Many retail stores let the children choose a small gift.

The inclusion of children in the March community was a logical extension of the motivation many people had for marching. A more secure future for one-year-old Alexa, the youngest Marcher, was what stirred her mother, Lynn Nadeau, a teacher. Donna Love, 57 years old and a self-proclaimed conservative from San Mateo, California, marched for her grandchildren and their future. Teacher Adeline McConnell of Denver said, "One reason I went on the March is because of the children's fears...My students kept bringing up the subject of nuclear war, and I simply felt I had to do something."

Children, of course, were not the only ones who learned important things from Marchers. Adults in churches, in civic organizations, in homes and local cafes looked—often with amazement—at charts showing the firepower of existing nuclear weapons and arsenals. One Marcher met, by chance, the pastor of a rural church who

Mary Giardina and her daughter Mariah

was actually unaware of the nuclear bomb tests in Nevada. Upset and angry, the minister asked for material to use in future sermons.

Marchers were educating themselves as well. Many had left Los Angeles with only a dim understanding of the nuclear arms race but became knowledgeable through reading in the March's mobile library of 4,000 books. We were also educating ourselves in Peace Academy. Inexperienced Marchers listened to more informed Marchers and attended talks by outside experts. This in-house education was optional but pervasive. Most Marchers welcomed the opportunity to learn.

Perhaps the most unusual visit from an outsider began at 1:30 one morning in rural Iowa when Marchers were awakened by an announcement that rock star Jackson Browne was in camp, "if anyone wants to get up." About 50 bleary-eyed Marchers assembled to hear Browne sing and tell them, "I think the issues of hunger and weapons are so closely related that when you start a song about hunger, it will end up about weapons and vice versa."

The following night in a sweltering gymnasium in Iowa City, Senator Tom Harkin, giving a major speech, told us and our supporters, "The Rambo administration thinks solely in terms of what it calls 'peace through strength.' Our answer is strength through peace. Instead of wishing for peace and preparing for war—a slogan we've all heard—it's time we started seeking peace by preparing for peace."

Guests such as Browne and Harkin were important. They were good for morale. It was easy to feel that the country didn't know and didn't care that every day several hundred people with a cause were packing up their belongings and their town to travel 15 or 20 miles down the road. Outside speakers assured us that we hadn't been forgotten, that what we were doing was indeed important and appreciated. In addition, speakers enlarged our understanding and knowledge, and some guests even taught skills in public speaking or gave information about how best to reach the public.*

For every "Go back to Russia!" yelled at us, we get a thousand "God-bless-you's."

–Lee Sims, Marcher

---

* By the time they reached Baltimore, Marchers had become so accustomed to public speaking about disarmament that 58 of them entered a competition for a place among those who would address audiences in the nation's capital. Each competitor had to post his or her speech for all to read and then deliver it before other Marchers. Balloting then determined which 12 speakers would represent the March before the public on the final day in Washington. One Marcher not present to compete was allowed to speak anyway. John Gordon, 74, had been forced out of the March by cancer.

September 10, 1986: Four hundred Marchers fast for 24 hours to support Vic Tolley, who is on an extended fast for atomic veterans.

Retired US Navy Admiral Gene LaRocque, director of the Center for Defense Information, told us to "strip the message down to its essentials. Of your goals, the test ban treaty is most important. Don't get drawn off trying to solve all the world's problems."

John Stockwell recounted some of his experiences as a high-level CIA official and warned us that at least three or four government departments may have sent agents into the March. Who these "government agents" might be became a matter for much speculation. Rumors centered around a few Marchers who always seemed to be involved when there was some kind of dissident activity, but no one ever found sufficient evidence to take action against a suspected provocateur.

Disruptions that seem to have been wholly spontaneous did occur. One day at the end of the summer, a busload of unconventionally dressed people stopped off at the March after attending a Rainbow Gathering, which is not to be confused with the Rainbow Coalition. The Gathering is an unpublicized annual get-together of thousands of people whom some would call hippies. The get-together goes on for days and involves alleged dope smoking and spiritual activities that are not in the mainstream of religious life. The Rainbow People decided they wanted to stay with the March. Evidence was lacking that they were committed to the cause of nuclear disarmament—or that they could pay their way or make real contributions to community life. And very real worries existed about drugs. Word went around that the Rainbow bus carried a lot of marijuana which the Rainbow People had harvested along the roadside and planned to sell in a big city.

Most Marchers did not relish the idea of adverse publicity that would come if narcotics agents should raid Peace City and find a duffel bag full of pot. But what to do? Without a search warrant, no one could legally poke around in the Rainbow bus. While adult officials of the March pondered and did nothing, one of the older kids took direct action. He entered the Rainbow bus, found the rumored duffel bag, took the contraband out into the woods and destroyed it. Adults no longer had to worry their heads about legal niceties.

Getting rid of marijuana was easier than getting rid of those who brought it into camp. Although never formally admitted, a few Rainbow People accompanied the March—and its kitchen—the rest of the way to Washington.

Whether or not the Rainbows did their share of work in camp or their share of walking on the highways, a noticeable number of people particularly in the later stages of the March did become "camp potatoes" (as in "couch potato") or "turnips" (because they seemed to turn up only for meals or media events). These vegetative folks were a drain on March resources, but they did not slow its steady progress.

As the warm days ended, we saw more and more of the death of the steel industry, and the devastation of human life that accompanied the closing of the mills had a deep effect on many. In Youngstown, Ohio, we found ourselves guests of unemployed steelworkers, some of whom sincerely supported the March with whatever meager resources they could muster.

The two-day stay in Youngstown gave us a chance to join in a Hispanic culture day parade. We were invited to speak in churches and schools and exchanged keys with the mayor. But at a rally of retired LTV steelworkers we became aware of a contradiction we had to learn how to deal with. The retirees, because of the bankruptcy of LTV, were threatened with loss of their health and life insurance benefits. The continuation of those benefits seemed to hinge on the survival of LTV's contracts for the stealth bomber and Star Wars.

The LTV retirees were concerned with their livelihoods and their own personal survival. Marchers were concerned with the survival of the planet; they wanted the arms industry shut down. Did this mean we were asking for increased unemployment in an industry where unemployment was already high? Clearly we who advocate nuclear disarmament must also have a plan for creating jobs, and many of us became aware of this need for economic conversion.

Some blue-collar hostility to the March came from the notion that we were independently wealthy people who could afford to stop working for nine months to walk across the country. A frequent taunt yelled from passing cars was, "Why don't you get a job?" A few of the older Marchers had been able to leave homes and jobs without serious financial loss, but many of those on the road had made considerable sacrifice in order to do what they were doing, and they considered marching the most important job they'd ever undertaken. So several shouted back, "We have a job and this it it!"

We went past miles and miles of shut down steel plants. They were like dead dinosaurs; there weren't even birds flying around. It was really weird.

–Pam Telleen, Marcher

During the March, it dawned on me that to bring peace about it would be necessary to work through our existing governmental structure. That means involvement and commitment to political process. Marching, walking or even crawling may have more human interest, but none of these will ever change institutionalized war mentality.

—Gerry Cartier, Marcher

A day's walk out of Youngstown, four parachutists, one of them a Marcher, floated out of the sunny sky, dropping unexpectedly into camp. Surprises were frequent, but some were less welcome than this diversion. The weather suddenly turned cold and rainy. As Marchers shivered in a town hall tent, they began to do serious planning for activities and events in Washington. The process went on endlessly in camp where Marchers were ill-informed about other plans, already well advanced, that were being firmed up by the volunteer GPM office and a committee working in the capital.

The border crossing into Pennsylvania was a hurry-up affair, for we had little desire to stand long in the rain and shout out the names of the ten states we had passed through. Better to keep going in the hope that there would be dry clothes and a dry tent at the end of the long walk.

A beautiful site in Shenley Park overlooking the city of Pittsburgh awaited weary Marchers as they finished the five-day trek from Youngstown. It had rained for three of the days, and legs long accustomed to flat terrain had had to adjust to the steep hills of Pennsylvania. Our rest day in Pittsburgh gave us a chance to dry out, and more than 100 of us attended an evening concert of the Pittsburgh Symphony. Free passes had been arranged by an orchestra member who was a brother of Marcher Josh Silver. Although showered and decked out in our best March clothes, we got stared at by the regular concertgoers as if we had just arrived from Mars.

The spectacle of economic collapse continued in Pennsylvania, just as we had observed it in the farming states of Nebraska and Iowa. East of Pittsburgh, we had new contact with labor problems in the steel industry as we passed through Homestead. There an eight-foot stone shaft bears this inscription: "Erected by the members of the Steel Workers Organization Committee Local Unions, in memory of the iron and steel workers who were killed in Homestead, Pennsylvania, on July 5, 1892, while striking against the Carnegie Steel Company in defense of their American rights."

Near the USX works in Homestead, Marchers and nearly 200 local people joined striking steelworkers in a rally protesting government policies. Mike Stout, representing United Steel Workers Local 1397, said to us that supporters of labor and peace "need to become one movement," because they have a common enemy in defense industries such as Rockwell International, Westinghouse and USX. From Homestead eastward the March passed other steel mills, silent, rusting, dead in their common grave—the Monongahela Valley.

This being November in an even year, an electoral campaign was in progress in Pennsylvania and, although the non-partisan March could not endorse any candidate, it could urge people to vote, and it could welcome the support of Rev. Bob Edgar, Democratic candidate for the US Senate. A number of Marchers took time off to do volunteer work as individuals in Edgar's office, thus reflecting an increased awareness of the importance of using the electoral process to fight against nuclear weapons. Marchers' help was not enough to win a Senate seat for Edgar, but as we came closer to Washington, we paid more attention to the need for finding a political solution for the political problem which the arms race represented.

The walk in western Pennsylvania took Marchers through small rural towns. At a campsite near Pittsburgh, we were kept awake most of the night by hecklers who shouted insults from speeding cars and shot off cherry bombs and firecrackers. A sympathetic editor in Ligonier wrote a supportive editorial in the local newspaper and later published a crusty response from Cordelia May, a member of the Mellon family. She wrote, "Since a march, even one comfortably buffered by bicycles, buses, and vans, does not afford its members much opportunity for fastidious personal grooming, one whiff of them should make nuclear weaponry obsolete and assure Russian capitulation to whatever demands we might make."

Cordelia May and a few others concerned themselves with how the Marchers looked and smelled. Many more people heard the message of the March and wrote letters to their local papers about issues that are seldom confronted in any community forum. Lively discussions about peace and nuclear issues appeared in the editorial and op-ed columns of newspapers across the country. Rebecca Swindell wrote to the *Rocky Mountain News* in Denver, telling how the March had raised her consciousness. "If the government will not listen to reason, then we have to have civilians who will stand up and say very loudly: 'Stop the bomb.'"

In the same issue, James Neil lambasted the Marchers as "a bunch of people out for a lark, who want to goof off for the summer," then added, "I'm all for peace, too, but the only way is to work, be productive, and pay taxes to keep this country strong."

135

In responding to a letter in the *Cleveland Plain Dealer*, Nancy De Nise thought the writer missed the point of the March when he wrote that it was miles away from solutions. Rather, she wrote, "It represents what is probably a desperate effort on the part of valiant, dedicated people to bring to the world's attention the fact that we are doomed as a planet if we cannot learn to be a peaceful planet....Many of us are like ostriches with our heads in the sand, hoping the terror of nuclear war will go away without any effort on our part."

Critics sometimes confused the goal—*global* nuclear disarmament—with unilateral disarmament. A reader of *50 Plus* magazine, Billy Sheets of Longmont, Colorado, accused the Marchers of having their heads in the clouds. "If we followed their advice, for unilateral disarmament on our part, we'd end up like those in Eastern Europe, Vietnam, Afghanistan and other countries overwhelmed by communism since World War II." The author of the article which stimulated the letter, Les Lindeman, replied, "None of the 50-plus people I talked with on the Great Peace March advocated unilateral disarmament. They favored a verifiable ban on arms testing and verifiable arms reduction." Unfortunately, such a correction did not usually accompany a misstatement.

Some Marchers expressed disappointment about the lack of national media coverage. It is true that the national media, after burying us in Barstow, ignored us until we reached the East Coast, but the GPM was front page news in most of the communities through which it passed, and the local television and radio stations usually informed their public about the arrival and schedule of the March.

Reading about the GPM or even seeing us on TV was no substitute for meeting us. Bill Oglesby, a professor at the University of Iowa in Iowa City, said, "I think we had a much deeper awareness of the issues after the March was here. When we had read about similar activities we hadn't paid much attention previously. When something like the March touches your community it makes you more aware, makes you think more intensely."

Without the local coverage, which the GPM media department often arranged, the local folks would, in most cases, have been unaware of our presence in their community.

If five million people went to Washington and stayed there till the end of the arms race, it would probably end in two weeks.

–Dr. William Caldicott in talk to Marchers

In Jennerstown, Pennsylvania, camp was set up near a dinner theater. The actors and stage crew took off half a day to talk with Marchers, and they sent Brooke Patterson, a theater technician, to walk with us as their representative the next day. Brooke remembered, "The town was talking about it for weeks. Considering the area, I thought the reaction was pretty good. The ones who were negative just saw them go by and were afraid."

In western Pennsylvania the road went up and down, up and down across the folds of the Appalachians. Nursing sore legs from the constant climb-and-descend, Marchers still kept a schedule of speaking in schools and churches. The music group Collective Vision and a March dance troupe performed at Pennsylvania State University. The women's band, Wild Wimmin for Peace played to a large audience in a church in Carlisle.

The United States Army has a war college in Carlisle, where officers learn about such things as Limited War in Theory and Practice, Low Intensity Conflict, and SDI Theory II. The GPM camped one night less than a quarter of a mile from the campus, and the March column made a stop at the gate. We gathered outside the main entrance and staged a "die-in"—that is, we fell to the ground as if killed by a nuclear explosion. As the "victims" lay motionless in front of several military police at the entrance, Nelda Trent recounted, to the sound of an ominous drum beat, the effects of a nuclear war. After several minutes, all except three of the demonstrators rose and marched on down the road. Those who stayed chose to trespass on the campus and were arrested.

The demonstration sparked articles and a critical editorial in the local newspaper, the *Sentinel*. But the Army's Public Information Officer, Lt. Col. Nick Hawthorne who witnessed the "die-in" said when he recalled it later, "I was very impressed by the discipline, orderliness, almost precision with which the March carried out the demonstration. I enjoyed their visit here. I wish they had been able to come onto the college and meet with the students and faculty and discuss these issues together." His superior had prevented that.

Roadsigns in this area indicated that Washington, D.C., was only about 100 miles away. Some people now argued in favor of bypassing New York and heading for the capital in order to arrive while Congress was still in session. Was it important to be there before Congress adjourned? Probably. But that would mean giving up exposure in New York City and Philadelphia as well as in the

No army can withstand the strength of an idea whose time has come.

–Victor Hugo

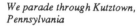

We parade through Kutztown, Pennsylvania

smaller communities along the way. November 15 had been advertised as the date of arrival, and thousands of supporters had made plans to arrive in Washington from around the country on that day. It was decided the date should not be changed. And so, leaving rural Pennsylvania behind, the March headed northeast through industrial Harrisburg, Reading and Allentown.

Outside Harrisburg, Mitch Snyder and Philip Berrigan joined the March at a lunch stop. While we sat in bleachers overlooking an athletic field, our guest speakers urged us to plan for a major action on November 15. They suggested civil disobedience would demonstrate a willingness to sacrifice. "I have a tremendous amount of respect for what you have done," Snyder said. "I believe in what you've accomplished so far. Make a statement that is the equivalent of the statement you made by walking across the country."*

Arrival in Kutztown, a small college community near Reading, brought out the Kutztown University marching band as well as a small airplane trailing a banner that read: WELCOME MARCHERS. Students hung out of dormitory windows and lined the street as the animated contingent passed in parade to the local site of Peace City.

At the Easton-Phillipsburg Free Bridge, Marchers exchanged Pennsylvania's royal blue flag for New Jersy's golden one. In less than a week, we would reach New York City. We would at last have conquered the continent on foot—and on time.

* Early in 1988, Mitch Snyder announced a march of the homeless from Los Angeles to Washington which would begin on March 1, 1988, the second anniversary of the beginning of the GPM.

Chapter VII

The East Coast At Last

October 23-25 : New York City
October 26-27 : Staten Island, NY
October 29 : New Brunswick, NJ
November 1 : North Philadelphia, PA

Excitement and anticipation grew as we walked through New Jersey, each day bringing us closer to New York City. Numbers also grew as supporters from around the country began to join us for the final leg of our journey.

In the expanding procession, many walkers had pinned to their jackets or caps small blue ribbons inscribed with the names and home towns of people they had met along the way. Early on, Katea Golub with the help of a few others had started the "blue ribbon project," asking friends of the March to wear one ribbon—indicating their desire for peace—and a second one to be taken by a Marcher to

They shall beat their swords into plowshares, and their spears into pruninghooks: nations shall not lift up sword against nation, neither shall they learn war any more.

–Isaiah 2:4

Washington. Thousands of citizens had responded, and now the bits of blue festooned the clothes of many Marchers.

Politicians in New Jersey had also joined in the blue ribbon project. Mayors in Montclair, Caldwell, Dover, Hackettstown and Phillipsburg all signed and added their ribbons to those of 160 other mayors who had already signed such ribbons. With election day close at hand, a number of candidates came to the March to mingle and speak.

Several Marchers had looked forward to meeting Dorothy Eldridge, longtime leader of New Jersey SANE and an enthusiastic supporter of the GPM. When the March neared her home in Nutley, word came that she had died suddenly. At a memorial service honoring her devotion to inclusive unity in the cause of peace, one of the speakers was a Marcher.

Then, as had so often happened, an unexpected event of another kind brought cheer. A celebrity guest who was scheduled to appear on the Phil Donahue Show on October 23—the very date of the GPM's New York arrival—suddenly cancelled. Donahue had been interested in the March but had already booked people for the days the GPM was to be in New York. Suddenly, the opportunity opened up for vast national exposure at a climactic moment for the March. Now—would Marchers help the show in this emergency? A signup sheet went around. The producers wanted 200 Marchers to fill the stage and studio at Rockefeller Center. Many of us were torn between this miracle and the desire to march in triumph across the George Washington Bridge into New York City.

At 5 a.m. on the morning of October 23, the Phil Donahue Show producers sent big busses to our New Jersey camp. They soon filled with sleepy but eager Marchers who had volunteered to be part of the all-March audience for that morning's nationwide telecast.

The rest of us gathered behind the flags and walked to a park overlooking the Hudson River and the New York skyline, waiting there for the police escort that would lead us across the George Washington Bridge to the city we would call home for four days.

A lone sailing boat was anchored in the Hudson River directly below us as we crossed the bridge. When word was passed along that it was Pete Seeger welcoming us from his boat, the *Clearwater*, people began to wave and shout.

At the end of the bridge members of the Living Forum, an artists' group seeking new ways to achieve peace, handed each Marcher a red apple as we stepped into the Big Apple. Also there to greet us were Casey Kasem, who had just completed a four-hour fund-raising broadcast for the March, members of the War Resisters League, local Presbyterian Church representatives and several classes of cheering youngsters from Public School 173.

A few steps and a few moments beyond, Marchers and supporters danced in the street to salsa music in Africa Square where we stopped for a brief rally. There we listened to Manhattan Borough President David Dinkins tell us, "In crossing this bridge today your 3,000-mile journey has come to a close, but the quest for peace must still continue." Where was Mayor Koch? A supporter of New York as a nuclear port, the city's mayor shunned the Great Peace March.

School children in New York City greet the March

141

While most of us were walking into the city, Phil Donahue was roaming up and down the aisles of the Rockefeller Center studio questioning and talking with Marchers of all ages and descriptions. They gave such a good account of themselves on the nationwide broadcast that $16,000 in contributions and many hundreds of letters from viewers poured into the GPM office in New York.

Appearing on stage were GPM supporters Peter Yarrow, Betty Thomas and Martin Sheen, along with Marchers Dick Edelman and Diane Clark. Ending the show on an upbeat note, Peter of "Peter, Paul and Mary" accompanied Marchers in singing "Blowin' in the Wind."

The Ubinas family gives us the peace sign as we rally in New York

Members of Riverside Church served lunch to everyone at Grant's Tomb on their way to camp on Randall's Island in the East River. Arranging for a campsite in New York had not been easy. Mayor Koch was not enthusiastic about the March, and officials under him refused to allow Peace City to use Central Park. As it happened, many Marchers and the majority of the Board of Directors were not particularly eager to camp in the park. Any demonstration there against the March could easily attract the media and detract from our main purpose. As well, it would be very difficult to protect the large number of campers from thieves who often roam the park at night. Randall's Island seemed much easier to make secure, and using the Triborough Bridge to Manhattan, Marchers could easily reach the city. So it was here, across from Harlem, that we set up our fading but still colorful little dome tents. Thirty or so others camped on the grounds of the Cathedral Church of St. John the Divine on 112th Street where they were more visible to Manhattanites.

Helpful though the police on the Randall's Island tried to be, they had problems. They could not distinguish Marchers in old clothes who had peace in their hearts from poorly dressed thieves who had larceny in theirs. Some losses could not be avoided in spite of efforts to beef up the GPM Peacekeepers to aid the uniformed police.

That evening, Marchers and their supporters gathered for an interfaith prayer celebration inside St.John the Divine, the largest Gothic cathedral in the world. On one side of the huge sanctuary hung three beautiful peace quilts, their red borders creating a striking contrast to the gray stone wall. One of the quilts bore embroidered portraits of American and Soviet children. Soviet women had sewn pictures of American children taken from photographs, and American women, pictures of Soviet youngsters.

While worshipers gathered, music by organist Paul Halley and saxophonist Paul Winter filled the cathedral, and the combined choirs of the Memorial Baptist Church later sang in gospel rhythm:

> *I don't feel no ways tired.*
> *I've come too far from where*
> *I've started from.*
>
> *Nobody told me the way would be easy.*
> *I don't believe*
> *He brought me this far to leave me.*

Episcopal Bishop Paul Moore spoke, and religious leaders from around the city took part in the service honoring the Great Peace March.

Next morning, accompanied by heavy police escort and a set of porta-potties, Marchers walked through Central Park, stopping briefly at the memorial to John Lennon. There we stood in a circle holding hands and sang "Imagine ," one of Lennon's songs.   At Columbus Circle we were joined by a group of supporters, some of whom were carrying huge white bird puppets.

The entire gathering continued through the city to Dag Hammarskjold Plaza near the United Nations. There, with several thousand New Yorkers who had come for the rally, we celebrated United Nations Day. Among the speakers were Rev. Jesse Jackson, who had first talked to us by telephone when we were in Las Vegas; Michio Kaku, professor of physics at the City University of New York, and Yoko Ono, widow of John Lennon, who later visited Peace City in New Jersey and gave the March $10,000. New York assemblyman Jose Rivera, representing two million Latino citizens, invited Marchers to come to the Bronx "to see what budget cuts can do to a community."

But it was television's Betty Thomas of *Hill Street Blues* who brought tears to the eyes of many Marchers when she told them how they had changed her life. "My life is so much better because of my time with you," she said. "I think about you in the morning, waking up, coming out of the tents, and I wish I were with you."

We can make it together. Together is the key.

–Yoko Ono

143

*June 12, 1982:
One million people
rally for a nuclear
freeze in New
York's Central
Park.*

Among the listeners at the rally were members of the March kitchen crew and the three City Managers. Usually they were too busy to take time off at this hour, but today they had crawled out of their sleeping bags very early at the Randall's Island site to prepare vegetables for the evening meal. While they were chopping away, several street people had wandered past the food truck, stopped in to nibble and stayed to help.

During the rally, a handful of Anarchists from the GPM and fellow Anarchists from New York paraded around the United Nations Plaza chanting, "No borders! No nations! No wars!" The UN Security guards arrested several of the demonstrators and turned them over to the New York City Police. No charges were filed, and they were released after being held over the weekend. Because of the disturbance, the United Nations was closed to visitors for two hours. This incident attracted attention from Long Island *Newsday* and resulted in some negative press for the GPM.

Generally, the March fared well with the New York based media. *People* magazine came out with a poignant article and twelve pages of photographs by Jeff Share, the biggest photo essay it had ever run. The largest New York newspaper, the *Daily News*, ran a cover story about the March in its Sunday magazine section. TV news programs carried stories, and radio station WBAI covered the March continuously throughout United Nations Day.

Meanwhile Philadelphians were being dramatically reminded of the March and its mission. Jerry Rubin (the Marcher, not the 60s protester), who had conducted current events discussions at many lunch stops on the March, had gone ahead to do advance work in Philadelphia where he once lived. There on October 2 Jerry had begun to fast. At the same time, in the home of the Declaration of Independence, he collected signatures to a World Declaration of Interdependence that he had unveiled earlier on the March. On UN Day he broke his fast and displayed to the press the 5,000 names signed on the 50-foot long Declaration which would soon be displayed at the concluding rally in Washington. In this action, as in many others, individual Marchers had taken the initiative but reflected the sentiment and spirit of most of us.

Next day, October 25, at still another New York rally, one of 14 being held simultaneously across the country, Marchers joined with the New York Action for Peace, Jobs and Justice. In front of the office of US Senator Alphonse D'Amato on 34th Street, this crowd made a vehement statement against nuclear weapons programs, in opposition to the Senator, and Jesse Jackson gave another eloquent address.

New York was a time for fun and high spirits, too. That evening, Marchers and a sprinkling of New Yorkers listened, clapped and sang to the music of Pete Seeger, Ronnie Gilbert, Odetta, Peter Yarrow and his daughter Bethany and others. March music groups Collective Vision and Wild Wimmin for Peace joined in the "Musical Celebration for Peace" which was held in St. Paul's Church in Harlem and also at nearby Columbia University, with performers shuttling back and forth between the two concerts. The audiences were not large. That night the GPM was up against unbeatable competition—the Boston Red Sox and the New York Mets in the sixth game of the World Series.

Lindy Flynn, Debra Osborne and 74-year-old Phyllis Rodin lead our parade across Brooklyn Bridge.

145

I was in the service in WW II and was on a train to go to Japan when the first bomb was dropped. We thought it was some kinda miracle. Then about 10 years later it began to hit home that the thing could fry the world. We would'a been better off without it.

–Owner of a GPM campsite

A Marcher-for-a-Day program—"Feet Against Arms" it was called—swelled the ranks of walkers to 878 the next morning. From City Hall through a part of New York that had not so far had a glimpse of the GPM, the procession crossed Brooklyn Bridge in the rain to lunch in Brooklyn's Prospect Park. By the time we reached the Verrazano Narrows Bridge which would take us across to Staten Island where we would camp, most were wet and tired—but not too tired to flash the two-fingered peace sign at passing motorists. City officials had threatened to keep Marchers off the bridge—which would have meant another Spirit Walk—but relented at the last moment.

On Monday, scores of Marchers boarded the Staten Island Ferry and New York subway trains and fanned out to elementary schools, high schools and colleges around the city. Thousands of students in classrooms learned first hand about Marchers and their mission.

Marshall Sclarow, an attorney and Marcher, talked to a class of adults who had only third-grade reading and writing skills. He recalled thinking, as he traveled to the school, that he might be wasting his time with such a group. But, he said, "I was amazed at the interest and enthusiasm of the students. I had a feeling they really became concerned. Later I got letters from many of them. They had all written to their Congresspeople and Senators." While Marchers were talking to school kids, our own March kids were on a field trip to the Statue of Liberty with their teacher for the day, Linda Cassasa.

On October 28 we left Greater New York and crossed into New Jersey again. As we proceeded in increasingly cold weather, we awaited news about the result of hectic fund-raising efforts that had gone on in New York. By the time we became guests of the students on the campus of Livingston College of Rutgers University in New Brunswick, the answer was in. New York, where March vehicles paid $1,000 to enter and leave, had been a media success but a financial disaster. The March had spent about $40,000 in fund-raising and publicity in New York City. Cash that came back to the March from this investment was about $20,000. This was exclusive of the spontaneous contributions that resulted from the Donahue Show.

With John Windle facilitating, the Board of Directors worked by flashlight, sitting on the chilly grass outside one of the Livingston

College buildings. Wearing warm jackets, Marchers stood around and listened to the bad news from New York. In the crowd was an inconspicuous man whom some of the veteran Marchers had seen before—but where? We recalled quickly when he wrote out a check to help tide the March over—a check that brought his total contributions up to $18,000. He was Michael Sherry, who had visited us months ago at the camp on the Nevada border near Whiskey Pete's. It was Sherry who had brought people out of their tents in the middle of the night and handed out packets of bills—$18 each. His latest gift would pay for enough gasoline and food to get us three days nearer to our goal.

At this troubled moment the Board faced a new problem. On October 29, with two critical weeks left—and in the midst of the worst financial crisis since Barstow—Mary Giardina and Peter Megginson resigned from the Board. This left only five members. Soon Board president John Records went off to do fund raising, but the key departments were all functioning. They could move the camp efficiently—if they could get the necessary cash.

In spite of the fact that the central policy-making body had been steadily weakened, and many Marchers still resisted being led, the March did continue with a semblance of order. Some help came from more than a few local activists in peace and justice organizations.

But the March continued mainly because it had responsible people in charge of the day-to-day operations. Generally speaking, these people were of two types. One type included peace-oriented, mature individuals who had well-ingrained work habits and who had had long experience caring for—being responsible for—the welfare of others. Among them were parents, teachers, middle-level executives in business or religious organizations and a few formerly in the military.

The second type included people who, though they had less experience, had learned skills as the March proceeded. Many had grown in their ability to assume responsibility, and the reality of the March made them aware of the need to use their skills.

In addition, these people, young and old, experienced and novice, knew there had to be give and take if we were to get to Washington. They seldom lost sight of that goal—or of their com-

Peace cannot be kept by force. It can only be achieved by understanding.

–Albert Einstein

147

mitment to peace. That allowed them to work together to keep the March going.

The process of working steadily, collectively, in an effort to contribute to the solution of an immense world problem, forced these Marchers to learn more and more about the realities of that problem—and of a host of lesser problems. One of these lesser realities they had to deal with was day-to-day living under very unusual, very stressful circumstances. Together they were starting to become a significantly expanded resource for the peace movement. They had become the seasoned activists who formed the sometimes fragile net that kept the March from falling apart as it continued toward Washington.

Discussion of what should go on as the March drew to a close involved all of Peace City as well as City Council. One member of the Council, Billy Lieb, has recalled this incident in the deliberations: "As we approached Washington several members of the Anarchists came to the City Council and threatened to take over the microphones at one of the concluding rallies if they were not allowed to speak. Their anger was somehow defused, and to the best of my knowledge their threat never materialized."

From the long drawn-out debates about what exactly should go on in Washington on November 15 and following the March's conclusion, 119 proposals had emerged! A number of these met considerable approval and were carried out. These will be described in Chapters VIII and IX.

Among suggestions that Marchers looked on with favor but did not act on—at least not at once—were: to organize a nationwide teach-in at public and private schools, colleges and universities; to set off on November 15 large-scale fireworks that would dramatize visually and audibly the firepower of World War I, World War II and present-day world nuclear arsenals; to march around the world, carrying symbols of peace, perhaps crossing the oceans on Greenpeace ships; to petition for a constitutional amendment banning nuclear weapons; to send aloft 54,000 black balloons, one for each nuclear weapon on earth; to set up a peace think tank—a Washington-based peace academy; to join with existing projects to encourage conversion of military facilities to peaceful uses.

I parked my March van briefly in front of a bakery. When I returned I found it completely filled with loaves of bread.

—Report from a Marcher

Among the 119 proposals were some—whimsical or wildly impractical—that were resoundingly defeated when put to a vote: a suggestion that the Marchers enter Washington walking backward; that they engage in a citizen's arrest of President Reagan; that they support a world-wide general strike to be called in support of nuclear disarmament. Of 238 Marchers who answered a questionnaire about proposals for the future, 19 voted, perhaps with tongue in cheek, to participate in armed revolution, if that became part of a GPM plan.

Several weeks before the end of the March, the Board of Directors had discussed the anticipated letdown Marchers would certainly feel after our Washington goal was accomplished and our community began to disperse. One of the ideas put forth to help with the transition to civilian life was a March directory so that communication between Marchers could continue. This first came up while we were crossing the vast stretches of the Midwest. Lesha Boggs, a housewife who was also an accomplished belly dancer, took on the project and began to collect names, addresses and identifying information (what were your main activities on the March? etc.)on forms that were circulated around camp. Dan Coogan improvised a photography studio, with natural lighting, set up in camp after each day's march. Over a period of several weeks, Dan, a photography student from Kent State University, captured each Marcher on film, a few at a time, day after day, and developed the prints in a darkroom in the back of a March bus.

Lesha's plan was to have the directory, *The Silver Thread*, printed in New York City just before the March arrived there, but Dan was still taking pictures, and the growing mountain of information hadn't been entered into the computer by late October. If the directories weren't ready to hand out in Washington they would have to be mailed at considerable expense.

Ashley Butler and Jordan Kohl began in earnest to put information into the busy, breakdown-prone computer, and Richard Polese, who had experience in publishing, took on the task of getting the directory into print. Barely two weeks were left. Richard enlisted Shaeffer Roemmele to hand-letter 700 names under the pictures (alphabetized by first name—since that's how most of us knew each other). The photographs were prepared overnight by a graphics house in Philadelphia, and the pasteups were done in a two-day blitz. A printer said he could meet the impossible deadline—if

The first thing the March did was to inspire me with hope again. Second, it gave me a vision of what community is and the potential of human beings. Third, it pushed me to further explore the connection between peace in my life and peace in the world.

–Steve Brigham, Marcher

149

Lesha would gamble on not seeing the proofs. If all went as planned the directories would be plated, printed, bound, trimmed, boxed and picked up in one week.

Let Richard recount the conclusion of this tale: "On November 13, our last site before Washington, *The Silver Thread* arrives in camp. True to Peace March traditions, the adventure is not yet over. I stash *The Silver Threads* in the InfoCenter trailer. We walk into D.C. and the St.Paul's College site. But, lo, the InfoCenter fails to arrive! And everyone is clamoring for their *Silver Thread*. The truck towing InfoCenter has broken down somewhere in Maryland... It finally comes in late at night. To make sure they won't disappear again, I stash two cartons in my tent, and the rest under the seats of the Merchandise bus. (Sally-Alice Thompson is a friend from New Mexico and it's her bus, and her word is as good as her bond.) Can anything go wrong?...Sure enough, they disappear again!

"After the climactic march through Washington and events on the Mall, Jackie Burch, who is helping with the distribution, and I return to the site to distribute the *Threads* to their eager owners—but the Merchandise bus isn't there. Not even Sally-Alice knows where it is. All I've got is the two cartons I tucked away in my tent—thank God! They're quickly gone, as rumors circulate about the bus being abandoned right in front of the Capitol. At daybreak, Sally-Alice and I grab a car and dash quickly downtown. Indeed, there's the bus, right in front of the Capitol. Mauricio Terrazas was driving and the entire electrical system failed right there. He worked out a deal with the D.C. cops to prevent it from being towed away until the next day. But it's locked, and no one seems to have a key. I jimmy a window, crawl in, and find the precious *Silver Threads*."

Richard and Sally-Alice get back to the site just as everyone is breaking camp. Most of the Marchers pick up their directories at the last possible moment, thus ending the saga of *The Silver Thread*.

Richard concludes, "This tale of *The Silver Thread* may not seem like an earthshaking event, yet it does seem to be serving the purpose Lesha Boggs envisioned: it has kept the whole Marcher family connected. Dog-eared, smudged and tattered, these blue bibles have turned out to be, indeed, 'the cord that keeps the soul connected to the body' of the Great Peace March."

Time seemed to be speeded up while we were advancing through the rain and cold of the East. Now, our ranks began to swell with many last minute Marchers, many of whom wouldn't be bothered with the formality of checking in at the Entry-Exit bus—people who had watched the GPM for months and wanted to share in its final days. And throughout camp, along with the growing anticipation, we were aware that the days left were precious few.

From the Exodus of Israel to the Long March of Mao Tse Tung, long marches have endured through time as a symbol of people's aspirations.

–Chris Satullo,
***The Express**, Easton, PA*

Chapter VIII

We Did It!

November 2-3   : Philadelphia, PA
November 5   : New Castle, DE
November 10-11   : Baltimore, MD
November 14-15   : Washington, D.C.

Red and gold leaves still clung to the trees as we made our way south through New Jersey, passing once again into Pennsylvania. Our reception in Bucks County, an area of strong Quaker influence, was warm. From there we marched into Philadelphia, birthplace of the nation, through Broad Street's impoverished neighborhoods.

"It was a spirited three days and one of the most successful things done in the last couple of years," said Billy Grassie, speaking as the Disarmament Coordinator for Friends Peace Committee, months after the March had visited Philadelphia. "The organizations we work with have experienced growth since the March. It was a fabulous organizing vehicle."

My feet are fine. Let's talk about arms.

—Message on T-shirt worn by Marcher

Sister Buffy Boesen, one of the City Managers

Billy Grassie also noted that, after November 15, a number of Marchers settled in Philadelphia. "We've benefited from having them here." The most lasting impact of the March, Grassie felt, was that it developed skills in a cadre of organizers.

What actually went on in Philadelphia that so impressed this Quaker activist? Except for the Independence Square candlelight rally, the Philadelphia stopover had not seemed to Marchers very different from those in some other cities. Perhaps the explanation is that what had become routine to us was far from routine for those with whom we came in contact.

Marchers were welcomed to the City of Brotherly Love on Sunday, November 2, by Mayor Wilson Goode at a small daytime rally. Following the event, at which several local politicians spoke, we paraded down Broad Street to Center City where we were joined by students from colleges in the area. Together, Marchers and students then walked to a lovely campsite in Fairmount Park where Philadelphians provided a potluck dinner. In the evening, many of us were guests at a classical music fund-raising concert put on by Philadelphia Musicians for Nuclear Arms Control.

Five thousand people, according to police estimates, turned out for the election eve rally and candlelight service the next night on the Mall near Independence Hall. Marchers and citizens were led in songs by Graham Nash and Peter Yarrow. Feisty Maggie Kuhn, the 83-year-old founder and leader of the Gray Panthers, who had addressed the Marchers before we left Los Angeles more than eight months before, urged us: "Tell the people to be careful with their vote. Remember, 54 cents out of every tax dollar goes to military spending." She gave a special award to the senior citizens—more than 50 of us—who had made the entire journey.

The route out of Philadelphia took us through suburban Swarthmore where arrangements had been made for the Swarthmore College Peace Collection to house the March archive. A rich accumulation of clippings, documents and records had been amassed over the miles and soon would become a resource for future research and reference. The next day, we bundled up as we crossed Delaware in rain and near freezing temperatures. We woke up in frost-covered tents most mornings now, but the thoughts of many began to turn to the separation we would soon face, and cold hands and feet were quickly forgotten.

November 10 we camped at Memorial Stadium in Baltimore. With the end of the March in mind we had a Hug Day. Everybody hugged everybody, acknowledging the strong family-like bonds that had grown with the months of walking together. And everybody kept avoiding intermittent downpours by ducking into tents which were scattered around the vast asphalt-covered parking lot beside the stadium. Camping on the grass of the playing field inside the stadium was not permitted, but the building provided shelter from wind and rain and also offered showers in rooms normally frequented by the Baltimore Orioles and visiting baseball teams.

Pete Seeger had come once more into camp, and when it was not raining he was out sitting on the asphalt, strumming his guitar. Peter Yarrow was in camp, too, making plans for post-March activities.

The success of a concert at Johns Hopkins University that night seemed, at first, very iffy. Some of the expected performers had to cancel. But, said Peter Yarrow, it turned out to be "the most amazing and wonderful concert of its kind—ever!" Musicians of GPM's own Collective Vision and Wild Wimmin for Peace sang with feeling and spontaneity. People from the audience were invited to share the stage and give impromptu performances. "The combination of the music and the poems of the Marchers with that of established performers made it unique," Peter said. "It was the musical expression of what the March seemed to be. It was filled with excitement, weariness, hope, tears, love and joy. The energy poured off the stage and in the end we experienced a feeling of binding solidarity."

On Veterans Day, November 11, Marchers soberly reflected on the civilian casualties of the militarization of the economy. At Johns Hopkins we saw a series of slides, which many Marchers had seen in Kutztown. The photos were taken by a Danish visitor, Jacob Holdt. His show, "American Pictures: A Personal Journey Through the American Underclass," graphically depicted the plight of the poor in this country.

That same evening, American Peace Test conducted a nonviolence training session, in preparation for a post-March civil disobedience action in which many planned to take part at the Department of Energy in Washington.

Bob Trausch and his son Zenon

Up to 50 masseurs will be at our site Sat., 11/14 for the first ever 'Massage for Peace.'
—*Peace City News,*
November 7, 1986

155

The last few days on the road saw more and more supporters joining the procession. They came into camp daily, almost hourly. The rest of us scurried around camp making last minute preparations to separate from Peace City and our friends as we continued southward.

On the morning of November 14, Marchers, now increased to about 1,800, put on their warmest clothes and strode to the border of the District of Columbia. There we mingled with those who had flown, bussed and carpooled in from all along the March route and other parts of the country as well. Chris Ball took charge of the final border crossing ceremony, asking everyone to line up shoulder-to-shoulder along grass that marked the D.C. line—by far the biggest border crossing in eight and a half months. Some held a big banner, the media were out in force, and all of us chanted in unison the names of all 15 states we had crossed. Then the whole assembly stepped into Washington.

"We did it! We did it!" many voices shouted, and many wept with elation—and relief. "We did it! We did it!" The chanting went on and on. Many of us had a sense of achievement such as we had never before felt. "We did it!" exulted Marcher Timothy Trujillo, "And just as they said we can't have a world without weapons, we will!"

Later that afternoon, Marchers set up their tents, many for the last time, on the grounds of St. Paul's Theological College in the city of Washington, D.C. We stood in long lines for dinner that night, having been joined by hundreds of supporters who would accompany the March through the streets and to the rallies the next morning. Kitchen chores were shared by devotees of the Krishna Consciousness movement, releasing the kitchen and dishwashing crews to concentrate on the next day's activities.

The biggest crowd since Los Angeles gathered behind the flags on the morning of Saturday, November 15. Walking down the middle of what were usually busy streets, we made our way toward Meridian Park. "When the marchers passed University Park Elementary School," wrote Saundra Saperstein in the *Washington Post*, "nearly 500 students, from kindergarteners on up, rushed out to see and touch the men and women who were celebrities to them. 'Welcome to Washington. Keep War Away,' one of the youngsters had written on a big white sign. Another sign read, 'Peace—A Weapon Greater than Anything.'" A cheering crowd welcomed us to the site of the first of three rallies, Meridian Park, also called

Malcolm X Park by the people who live near by. Around the perimeter thoughtful volunteer organizers in D.C. had placed signs bearing names of the states, thus giving people a chance to find visitors from their home towns. Friends and families held warm reunions. While Mayor Marion Barry welcomed everyone, many Marchers gathered a few hundred feet away to say some last good-byes. Someone in the group yelled, "Let's have a group hug!" Scores of bodies hurtled toward each other into a clump that tottered dangerously for a moment, then settled into a tearful swaying bunch of friends.

Back into the streets again, we walked in deliberate silence down 16th Street toward the White House, with the wail of a lone bagpipe and the slow beat of the Buddhist drums the only sounds. Occasional pedestrians on the sidewalk stopped and looked in some surprise at the eloquent, soundless mass of people filling the street from curb to curb. Uniformed Black guards in a government office building stood at windows and gave the two-fingered peace sign.

Pete Seeger, Peter Yarrow and Jim Scott were strumming and singing "This Land Is Your Land"as the crowd arrived in Lafayette Park across from the White House. Mistress of ceremonies, actress Lindsey Wagner, held up her 10-week-old son as a sample of the future for which we had been marching.

True to the promise he made in Iowa City, Senator Tom Harkin was there to meet us. He read a proclamation of congratulation to the Marchers which had been signed by 14 senators, and he went on to say, "Our security in the nuclear age is a false security, based on a foundation of fear of universal suicide.

"Pentagon planners, driven by Richard Perle—a kind of yuppie Dr. Strangelove—have raised even higher the stakes of the nuclear arms race—right up into space.

"Star Wars, with its $1 trillion price tag and its Buck Rogers technology, now stands between a comprehensive arms control agreement and a costly more expanded nuclear arms race."

Congressman Ed Markey of Massachusetts spoke about the present as he recalled a grim moment in the American past: "While slavery was the great issue of the previous century, the most radical injustice ever perpetrated on this planet has occurred in this century.

Can words adequately express our concern about nuclear weapons? Hiroshima's dead and the unborn future watch us silently. We are walking for them...we are speaking out in silence.

—Message on card passed around during the silent march

157

It is the handing over of the power of nuclear weapons to the hands of a small number of white men…who…control the destiny of this planet." Then speaking directly to the Marchers, he said, "You are the soul, the spirit and the heart of what this country stands for, and that is an end to the sword of Damocles hanging over our planet."

Carl Sagan condemned Star Wars as a scientific absurdity. But, he insisted, "Reason will ultimately prevail [and bring an end to the arms race]. The alternative is that no one will be left to do the reasoning." In conclusion, he said, "I salute you, I welcome you, and I assure you that there is a change happening at this moment…and we are going to see a significant change in U.S. policy on nuclear weapons." (The full text of Dr. Sagan's speech appears in the appendix.)

Dr. Michio Kaku, the nuclear physicist who had spoken to us on United Nations Day, joined Major General Jack Kidd, USAF (ret.), in pointing out that Star Wars is an offensive, not a defensive weapon.

On this concluding day, at one of the three rallies, Marcher John Gordon rose, looking gaunt but determined. Cancer had driven him from the March back in Colorado, and he knew, and so did we, that he did not have long to live. Now he had flown from California to celebrate with his friends. Here is his valedictory contribution to the March:

> Mr. President:
> We do not need more *nuclear weapons.*
> What we do need is *new clear thinking.*

> Mr. President:
> You are a decent and honorable man, but you are wrong when you say Communism is the enemy.

> Mr. President:
> *COMMUNISM IS NOT THE ENEMY.*
> *HUNGER IS THE ENEMY*—and we can help alleviate the hunger by sharing more of our bounty with an undernourished world.
> *For we are one human family.*

> Mr. President:
> *SOCIALISM IS NOT THE ENEMY. DISEASE IS THE ENEMY*—and with a fraction of the

November 15, 1986: Camilla Taylor, a 15-year-old who began a peace petition when she was 12, called on Reagan and Gorbachev to listen to the children. "We will not let ourselves be brushed aside," she said firmly.

money we spend on armaments we can eliminate most of the diseases that plague humankind. *For we are one human family.*

Mr. President:
MARXISM-LENINISM IS NOT THE ENEMY. POVERTY AND ILLITERACY ARE THE EMENY!
and we can redirect our resources and intellect toward the eradication of these twin scourges that make life so hopeless for so many. *For we are one human family.*

Mr. President:
OTHER NATIONS, RACES AND RELIGIONS ARE NOT THE ENEMY. INTOLERANCE IS THE ENEMY,
and we must learn to understand and respect our diversity. *We are one human family.*

And finally, Walt Kelly's cartoon character "Pogo" said it best when he said:

We have met the enemy, and he is us! But with *new clear thinking*, Mr. President, we can overcome all these "enemies" without going to war. Only then can we call ourselves truly civilized. *

Mr. President—Ronald Reagan—did not hear John Gordon's words nor did he acknowledge our presence in front of the White House. One or two Marchers slipped through the cordon of police guards surrounding his executive residence, to leave their calling cards: they tied their worn marching shoes to the iron fence around the White House.

With ceremonies at Lafayette Park completed, the crowd slowly made its way to the Mall where the walkers separated into two columns as they took their last steps together around the Reflecting Pool. Gathering at the Lincoln Memorial, we heard our old friend Holly Near welcome us with her song, *The Great Peace March*:

> *Peace can start to move in just one heart*
> *From a small step to leaps and bounds*

November 16, 1986: About 60 Marchers and supporters wrap 20,000 signed Blue Peace Ribbons around the Washington Monument.

* John Gordon died April 26, 1987

159

A walk becomes a race for time
And a brave child calls out to the crowd . . .

We will have peace,
We will because we must,
We must because we cherish life.
And believe it or not,
And daring as it may seem,
It is not an empty dream
To walk in a powerful path
Neither the first nor the last Great Peace March*

Then Marchers who had been selected by their fellow Marchers to speak, stepped to the microphone, one by one. Their words, brief but poignant, came from the heart and from the many miles. Lucia Darvill, a 12-year-old from Australia, Lynn Nadeau standing with her one-year-old daughter, Alexa, on her shoulders and Tracy Bartlett, a singer with Wild Wimmin for Peace, were three of the speakers.

As twilight came and the Rev. Jesse Jackson and others spoke and sang, small clusters of Marchers made their way to the nearby Vietnam Memorial. There at America's unforgettable monument to the futility of war, some left their candles at the foot of the columns

Candle light rally around the Reflecting Pool, November 15, 1986

of names and remembered the Americans and Vietnamese who would never again see their families. One wrote on a blue ribbon given him by a supporter miles and months before: "We will remember, and we will work to see that this never happens again. Love, A Great Peace Marcher."

Franklin Folsom, the eldest Marcher, had also spoken on that final day:

We have crossed the continent
    to save life—
    all life.

We have walked to Washington
    to save ourselves—
    to save us all.

We march to Congress announcing
    "You persons in power must guard our lives—
    and your own.
    You can do this by ceasing to take money from us
    and giving it to the makers of nuclear weapons.
    You can do this by not killing us slowly
    with deadly debts, escalated to pay
    escalating manufacture of nuclear weapons
    that will kill us instantly."

We approach the Capitol
    voicing the will of our fellows.
    We utter the cry of millions
    "Stop testing!
    Stop Star Wars!
    End the arms race!
    End this nuclear madness!"

We stand before our President, insisting
    "Talk, talk and talk some more
    with the Soviet leader.
    He wants to live, just as you do.
    The Soviets want a world for children,
    just as we do.
    We all want this, not a Star Wars umbrella
    that is a sword in disguise.
    We all want life, not Armageddon.
    Talk, Mr. President. Talk and agree on life."

We knock on your door Mr. President.

We have come to reason with you
    and to let you count
    the countless people who have sent us.

Mr. President, we have crossed
    all of our country
    and we will be heard—
    and heeded.

Mr. President, we started our March
    at three minutes to midnight
    on the atomic clock.
    We intend to close our March
    at high noon
    on the clock of the life-giving sun.

The Hiroshima Flame, which had accompanied the March all the way from Los Angeles, played its role in the closing ceremony. From the flame, thousands of people lit candles and set them afloat on the Reflecting Pool. The small lights glowed in the dark, each one promising that the work of the March will go on until nuclear weapons are no more, and the flame of Hiroshima need burn no longer.

From Los Angeles to Washington, D.C., by way of New York City, Marchers walked 3,701 miles.

Chapter IX

Was It Worth It?

Personal transformations
Expanded peace activities
Changes in communities
Spinoffs from the GPM
Changes on the international scene

What did the Great Peace March *really* accomplish? Was the expenditure of time, money and effort on the part of several thousand Marchers and March supporters justified? Did the effort to take the message to the people prove successful? And how can one measure the results? These questions have no easy answers, but the search, for some, produced fascinating responses from across the country.

To begin an evaluation of the March, I (*C.F.*) retraced our route, from Los Angeles to Washington, for four-and-a-half months in the summer of 1987. I talked with hundreds of people, some who

You were out there and visible, and even if you affected people only subliminally, it was important. Your presence helped underscore that people are willing to take some action for something they believe in.

—Suzy Marks,
Chair,
California Freeze Voter

watched the March from a distance, some who visited Peace City and got to know Marchers, and others who supported the March with food, shelter, money and advance work preparing for the passage of the March through their community. In addition, I talked with Marchers—people who had walked all the way, others who had been inspired by the March and decided to join after seeing us, and folks who walked with us for a short time.

Our scientifically oriented society expects results to be expressed in numbers—how many? how much? how long? But as we are reminded by Marilyn Ferguson in her study of late 20th century grassroots phenomena, *The Aquarian Conspiracy*, important elements of life cannot be measured. She asks, "How big is an intention? How heavy is grief, how deep is love?" And I asked, "How did the March change you, your family, your community?"

Ram Dass, who walked with and visited the March said, "The March moved the heart." I found that it moved the hearts not only of those who observed it, but also of those who took part in it.

How else can one explain responses of Robyn Singleton, the reporter from the *Iowa City Press Citizen*, who was sent to cover the March for her paper and was so taken by what she saw that she quit her job and joined us? Or Emily Crawford, a 17-year-old Marcher whose mother said, "The big difference after the March was that she had changed in a basic way. She liked herself."

Many people realized, as did a supporter from Los Angeles, that "the Marchers were personally revolutionized, that for the rest of their lives they're more powerful persons. There is that block of trained persons out there that people know were Marchers."

What can account for the transformation among Marchers that so many have recognized? Living in a community close to the earth, leading a simple life, finding meaning in our lives by working for a cause bigger than the next paycheck, learning tolerance and acceptance—all these things and more played a part in the changes many of us experienced.

When we arrived in Washington on November 15, we realized that our job was far from finished. "The only thing that's over is the walking," said Carole Schmidt, 25, of Chicago. After leaving the nation's capital, Marchers fanned out across the country to join existing peace groups, to begin new projects within the peace movement and to continue talking, teaching and walking for peace.

In our home towns we found that people were interested in hearing our stories. Because we had walked with the GPM, we were asked to speak in churches, schools and civic organizations and on TV and radio programs. People who had never spoken in public before were using skills they had developed on the March. Speaking about peace had become easy.

Marchers turned up in SANE/FREEZE offices as valued employees and volunteers. They found jobs with Physicians for Social Responsibilty, Women's International League for Peace and Freedom, Nebraskans for Peace, American Peace Test and many other peace and justice organizations. And wherever they went they were welcomed as trained, committed and educated activists.

Monica Green, executive director of Greater Cleveland Freeze and new co-chair of SANE/FREEZE said, "We have two new staff members from the March. They came to us with organizational skills and the proper education about the issues."

The GPM inspired many Marchers with ideas for what they can do as individuals to continue to work for peace. Alex Smith, an ex-minister from Fullerton, California, decided to coordinate a letter-writing campaign in behalf of a test ban. Ed Fallon, the GPM's state coodinator for Iowa, set up the Des Moines Campaign for Nuclear Disarmament after the March was over. His group concentrated on canvassing in the Des Moines area. He was inspired to begin the organization as a result of his March experience and closing of the local Freeze office.

After the March ended, a group of about ten settled in Boulder, Colorado, and decided to organize action against the nearby Rocky Flats plant where triggers for nuclear weapons are manufactured. Under the name *Shut Down*, with Sherri McCutchen and John Chanin as the active planners, the group organized monthly walks to and vigils at the plant. Then in August 1987 their first major demonstration took place. More than a thousand protestors blocked the entrance to the plant, shutting it down for five-and-a-half hours, and 320 were arrested. Further demonstrations were planned.

We have gone on piling weapon upon weapon, missile upon missile like men in a dream, like lemmings heading for the sea.

—George Kennan, former Ambassador to Moscow

In the pre-caucus days of 1988, two Marchers, Pattie Ankrum and Bruce Bishop, went on a speaking tour in Iowa urging people to vote and reporting on the GPM and the American-Soviet Walk in which they also took part. Earlier they spoke to more than 100 audiences in eight other states under the sponsorship of the Mennonites. Of the GPM, Pattie said, "It made thousands into peace activists. It radicalized a lot of people."

Two other Marchers, Madeleine Turner and Laura Fischrup, began publishing *Take Action*, a networking calendar. Their purpose was to list the peace and social justice actions taking place in the far western United States and to give information about ongoing vigils and direct action in other areas.

Many Marchers stayed in Washington two extra days to take part on November 17 in a blockade of the Department of Energy, which oversees the nuclear tests in Nevada. The action, planned by the American Peace Test, SANE, the national Freeze campaign, the Jewish Peace Fellowship and individual Marchers, began with the blowing of a ramshorn and ended with the shutdown of the Department of Energy and the arrest of 137 people, the majority of them GPM veterans.

Marchers continued to be unofficially represented on the international scene by their ceremonial mayor, Diane Clark, who has described herself as leading a conventional life before the March. In follow-up activities she traveled to the Vienna International Peace Dialogue, the World Conference Against Atomic and Hydrogen Bombs in Japan, to Moscow where she met with members of the Soviet Peace Committee, and to Poland for the International Peace Conference, all in 1987. She was named Woman of the Month by *McCalls* magazine in April of that year.

Creativity was never in short supply in the March community, and the results of that creativity have surfaced in many areas since the GPM ended. Cathy Zheutlin filmed a very moving video documentary, *Just One Step: The Great Peace March* , while she was part of the March. Jeff Share, a 24-year-old photographer from Los Angeles, followed the March across the country with cameras clicking and was rewarded with four major photography prizes and two major exhibits of his March pictures. Jeff and *Los Angeles Times* writer Kathleen Hendrix put together a photo essay book on both the GPM and the American-Soviet Walk.

Collective Vision, one of the musical groups to spring from the March, went on a nationwide tour in 1987, spreading the words of peace through their music. They were also part of the American-Soviet Walk in June and July, 1987 and performed at the July 4 rock concert in Moscow at the conclusion of the walk.

Marchers found that their vision of the world had expanded and their place in it had changed after walking across the country. Don Billen, an electrical engineering student at the University of Missouri before the March began, realized that his intended career would probably lead him into some aspect of weapons manufacturing. So he is changing both his career goals and his college.

Willie Fragosa, who says he was on the "materialistic fast-track" selling solar panels in Los Angeles before the March, said, "I'll still be in sales, but now I'll be selling peace." He's giving up his dream of being a land baron.

Walking across the United States, talking with the American people, gave Marchers a positive attitude toward the country whose official policies often run counter to their beliefs. Don Billen realized that his participation on the March had given him "a newfound patriotism—a belief, not in the government, but in the people of this country, in their wonderful goodness."

Marcher Elizabeth Fairchild said, "I learned to love the American people. I was so impressed by the people we met and talked to, how kind they are. Whenever we needed things, people would come and help us, regardless of how they felt about what we were doing."

Many Marchers—and others—came to believe that Americans need to redefine patriotism. Randy Kehler, writing in *Nuclear Times* (Nov./Dec. 1985), says that many in this country feel caught between conscience and culture. The cultural attitude is that protest and dissent are unpatriotic. At the same time, a large majority of Americans would like to see nuclear weapons eliminated. The March brought this contradiction to the fore in the minds of some onlookers. Since, in the nuclear age, the interests of the United States and the rest of the world can't be separated, Kehler contends that patriotism cannot any longer consist of blind allegiance or of thinking that the United States is better than any other country. Dissent, he says, is patriotic when citizens are protesting policies

167

Show me who makes a profit from war and I'll show you how to stop the war.

—Henry Ford

that threaten the survival of everyone. Many Marchers came to realize that, in order to survive, our allegiance must be to the earth and to all peoples on it—an all-encompassing patriotism.

Personal growth was a frequent result of being on the March. Sue Daniels, a 47-year-old teacher from Fullerton, California, says of the changes in her life at the end of the March, "I'm more of a risk-taker now. I'm more comfortable living with less. I've lost some of my naiveness. I'm not sure what form my life will take next, but I do know I'm going home a stronger person."

Aleida VanDyke, 67, had been too retiring to speak before people. Now she says, "I'm explaining amendments, the test ban and the summit to groups. I'm not shy anymore."

Crystal Constantine was ten years old when she told her parents she wanted to join the March. Although resistant at first, they finally gave their consent, and her father noted afterward, "The March made Crystal realize she was a person—not just a kid. She learned that her opinions are valid. It matured her intellectually and socially." Crystal was further reminded that her beliefs are important when she was among 20 children from around the world who were invited by a consortium of peace organizations to be on hand in Washington on December 7, 1987, at the time of the Reagan-Gorbachev summit.

The experience of living in community accounts for many of the changes in the minds and hearts of Marchers. Scott Peck, writing in *The Different Drum*, describes a community as a group of people who meet each other without the usual defenses and who value the diversity among themselves. The March community began to form in the remote California desert after PRO-Peace had pulled out, and we were left with little but our few personal possessions and tents. A true crisis. And, as Dr. Peck notes, communities frequently arise spontaneously amid a crisis. But they seldom last. Once the crisis is over, they tend to dissolve.

Perhaps the March community survived because there was almost always a crisis of some kind. Or perhaps it persisted because many worked at keeping it alive. And maybe it had something to do with the consensus form of government, with the policy of inclusiveness, and with the respect for the rights of individuals. Also the physical acts of walking and camping together were strong factors in the bonding process that took place. Most Marchers would agree that the sense of community was much more alive in Washington than it had been in Barstow eight months earlier.

For many, living in Peace City had been their first taste of being part of a true community.

When asked what it was that appealed to him and prompted him to walk with the March across Iowa and Illinois, high school student Ben Connelly said it was "the spirit of togetherness." And it was the sense of "being at home" her first day with the March that caused Robyn Singleton to quit her newspaper job and join. Iowan John Shumaker, who came on in Pennsylvania, also declared, "This is where I've always belonged—with these people in this work." Shumaker would walk from Leningrad to Moscow the next year.

Perhaps it is not surprising that most of the Marchers refer to the "Peace March family" as an ongoing community and meet and visit one another often. But the phenomenon goes deeper than simply similar opinions or a shared goal; living closely with one another through discomfort, conflict, disappointments, triumphs and more than a handful of miracles seemed to have given them a durable bond of tolerance and love for one another. As an aid to keeping Marchers in touch, Bill O'Neill has published *The Silver Thread Update*, which informs the March family of changes of address, events in which marchers are participating, as well as marriages, births and deaths.

Parents of children who joined the March sensed a feeling of comfort and acceptance that helped them make the decision to allow their children to become Marchers. "It was a wonderful community to step into," said the parent of a 17-year-old. "It's why we felt fairly secure in saying, 'Fine. Go.'"

"We went to see the March before we decided to let Crystal join it," said Susan Constantine of her ten-year-old daughter. "The March had a great feeling of openness. The peace movement has a tendency to be heavy and judgmental, self-righteous. The Marchers were unpretentious. Living together day-to-day put them in touch with the people on the street. I think the March was the seed of a very different direction."

Marchers were changed and so were their families. Liz Vance,

The love of one's country is a splendid thing. But why should love stop at the border?

–Pablo Casals

17, returned to her home in Oberlin, Ohio, with a packet of information about the arms race. Her father, Philip, read the material and realized he'd inherited some stocks that weren't related to peaceful endeavors—stocks in corporations that were involved in military work. "So I proceeded to sell them. And it did hurt. I remember selling IBM, AT&T, GM. It was fun doing it, but at the same time it was frightening."

Carole Schmidt told about her grandmother, a Reagan supporting, conservative Republican, who came to camp and "had to see everything."

"She went back to Jacksonville and called the press. She's a very influential woman down there. So the press came and she told them the story about the March and her granddaughter. Then she wrote a letter to Reagan telling him that she was a conservative Republican, but she thought he'd better listen to her granddaughter because she was right about nuclear weapons.

"I changed her mind," said Carole, "and it was great to see that happen."

Spectators along the route who took the time and trouble to talk with Marchers, and supporters or even uncommitted Good Samaritans who provided a meal, a shower or a place to sleep were—in many cases—deeply affected.

Jean Shelby, an English teacher at Avon Lake High School in Ohio, said, "I never really thought about peace until I spent an evening in Peace City talking with Marchers." As a result of that brief contact, Jean drove to Washington the weekend the March arrived. Later she traveled to Los Angeles and dropped into a bookstore where amid "lots of really neat things," she found a "peace pole" (a four-foot post with "May Peace Prevail on Earth" printed on it in four different languages). She carried it back to Avon Lake where she planted it on the school grounds. "I hope the pole makes some people stop and think about what's really going on today.... At least I'm not fading into the woodwork so much anymore. I'm making a contribution."

A chance meeting with the March on Loveland Pass in Colorado inspired a Pennsylvania dentist, Edward Bromall, to round up his

You perhaps changed the course of history. Of course you changed the lives of the people who walked.

—Rev. Albert Cohen,
Campus Pastor,
California State University,
Los Angeles

staff and several colleagues to clean Marchers' teeth when we passed through Philadelphia months later. "Within my own staff everyone had a lasting impression," said Dr. Bromall. "It really raised our consciousness about the issue. I've never been one who has been in organizations. I always wanted to see the results right away when I did something, and here were all these people doing something and not knowing what the results would be. I gained a great deal of strength from that. It helped me want to participate more. I've written to my legislators several times since then. It had a very positive effect on me."

The effect of the GPM on those who interacted with us was evident in the earliest days. "Bible Bob" came to heckle us in Los Angeles when the March began. Through a loudspeaker in his panel truck he kept up a constant harangue, plugging his fundamentalist view of the world's troubles—and criticizing the March. For several days "Bible Bob" followed our column and preached to us—and against our mission. But Marchers were courteous, and "Bible Bob" began to listen some and talk less. When he bade us farewell as we headed into the desert, he said he was for us, but warned us to avoid fornication because "it weakens the legs."

A young reporter from the high school newspaper in Parachute, Colorado, asked to interview Jolene DeLisa. He had chosen a passionate and outspoken woman in her 50's as his subject. As they talked, he told her that his father had been a Marine, his brother was a Marine and he was going to be one, too. It was the patriotic thing to do, he said. Then he began to cry. He said that the March had confused him. Seeing the Marchers and talking with Jolene had challenged his beliefs. How many others across the country were challenged in a similar way?

"I remember seeing you coming up the frontage road thinking you were coming to wake up people like me," recalls David Optekar. In 1986, David, 38, was selling real estate in Glenwood Springs, Colorado. He remembers reading about the March in a Denver paper some time before we arrived in Colorado. "I wasn't open to it at all. I was shut down about the whole issue. I thought, 'They're a pain in the neck.' Before the March I was of the opinion that we had to be stronger than Russia. That attitude began changing during meditation when I kept getting the message that I should do massage for you folks. I tried to shove the thought away, but it kept returning."

171

So David rounded up some friends in Glenwood Springs, and they went down to camp to knead the sore muscles of weary Marchers. After spending two days in Peace City, David says, "I wrote a letter to the *Glenwood Post* about the March. I was afraid I'd go to sleep again. The letter helped me come out of the closet about how I felt. It was scary, but invigorating. The message you were carrying, the desire for peace, is in everyone of us, and you woke me up. It wasn't all the talking. It was your presence."

The young reporter's experience and David's story point up several steps in what is usually a fairly long process of attitudinal change. The high school student was confronted with a new idea about patriotism. A seed was planted in his mind. David received repeated exposure to a point of view different from his own in the two days he spent in camp. He was able to accept the new ideas, and to make sure he would hold onto them, he went public in the local paper.

Obstacles to accepting new ideas are very real. But there is additional resistance to dealing with the threat of nuclear weapons. It is an enormously frightening and overwhelming issue which forces us to look at death—not only our personal death but death of the entire planet, of everyone and everything we know. The presence of the GPM brought the issue out into the open in communities across the country, and the Marchers were showing, by their presence and commitment, that others needn't sit by helplessly while governments manufacture weapons for our possible extermination.

Of course, not every hawk along the way was transformed into a dove because the GPM walked down a nearby highway or camped in a nearby park. The expectation of educating people was part of David Mixner's vision which the GPM inherited when PRO-Peace folded. The March never had the money or connections that Mixner planned on when he prophesied that thousands of people across the country would visit Peace City's "mural-festooned, environment-friendly model community" where experts and Hollywood personalities would educate the masses. The GPM had no glamour to draw the curious. Instead, some people were drawn to it by tales of "weird hippies" entering town. Others came to see what kind of folks felt so strongly about a cause that they would take nine months from their lives to walk across the country. A few came for some personal reason; some only to see what was going on, or because they got an

Warfare is just an invention known to the majority of human society by which they permit their young men either to accumulate prestige or avenge their honor.

–Margaret Mead

172

invitation from a friendly Marcher. These magnets were not compelling enough, however, to draw multitudes.

Those who did come, for whatever reason, were often captivated by what they saw and often stayed for a time to talk with Marchers. One-on-one contact worked often and worked well.

Jack Settle, a woodworker at Living History Farms outside Des Moines, Iowa, visited with Marchers while we were camped at the Farms. "It was an intense consciousness-raising event for me. I had always seen the peace movement as the fantasy of a few decent but deluded people. For the first time, after seeing the peace march, I felt peace was possible and that speaking out might make a difference"

A very natural outgrowth of the GPM continues to be any number of similar but smaller marches and walks in this country and abroad. Nearly all have been organized by people from the GPM. Meg Gage, executive director of the Peace Development Fund, said, "The March has spawned marches all over the country. They make sense to me. They have a quality of witness that isn't a demonstration and that appeals to a lot of people."

Many communities across the country had concurrent one-day marches on November 15, 1986, when we arrived in Washington. A particularly successful effort was carried out in Salt Lake City where 957 local citizens participated in a two-and-a-half-hour event. A graphic artist, Donna Kiddie, organized this march. She had never done anything in the peace movement before, but that experience launched her into an activist role. She followed her November 15 project by participation in the 1987 American-Soviet Walk.

Soon after the conclusion of the GPM, and with the Great Peace March as a model, the National Mobilization for Survival and the Florida Coalition for Peace and Justice sponsored a three-week march through Florida, ending at Cape Canaveral on January 17, 1987. The Florida march then went on to protest against the first test of the Trident II nuclear missile and resulted in the arrest of many GPM Marchers. They, along with other demonstrators, were jailed for committing civil disobedience.

A high school student from Omaha, Brian Peterson, was one of those jailed. He had traveled to Washington for the final day of the

Most everywhere we went (in CA and NV) we ran into someone who was doing something because of the March.

–Ted Gies,
Peace Movement
Assessment Project

March in 1986. "I was influenced to go on the Florida March by going to Washington," he recalls. "The Marchers made me much more aware of having to take a risk. I spent three weeks marching in Florida and then I spent 15 days in jail. For that I lost a semester of school. Seeing all the Marchers and the rallies gave me energy to say, 'Yes, I want to do this.'"

The idea for a walk in the Soviet Union was born during the final weeks of the GPM. Marchers traveled to Moscow on three different occasions to set up arrangements with officials of the Soviet Peace Committee.* Despite a short time in which to prepare, 230 Americans and 200 Soviet citizens took part in the unprecendented American-Soviet Walk in June and July, 1987, from Leningrad to Moscow, to promote the cause of peace. Seventy of the Americans had been participants in the GPM and many of the other Americans were inspired to join because of contact with the GPM. The organizing group in the US called itself International Peace Walk and announced plans for more bilateral walks in both the USSR and the US in 1988. The key figures in the International Peace Walk are all GPM veterans. (For address see appendix.)

A dramatic moment came at the conclusion of the American-Soviet Walk when, for the first time ever, a Soviet participant, carrying an American flag, and an American with the Soviet flag strode together through Red Square. Later both groups were honored with the largest rock concert ever held in the Soviet Union, which included top name performers from both countries. As it turned out, the concert got far more press in the West than did the American-Soviet Walk itself.

Other Marchers took part in a peace walk in New Zealand in 1987. Most were nationals of that country, but two, Paul Ziegler and Susan De Lettera, were from the United States. In Australia, an action of a different kind included Australian Trevor Darvill of the GPM. On June 9, 1987, the Greenpeace vessel Vega took up position in the mouth of the Brisbane River to engage in a symbolic blockade, as the nuclear frigate the *USS Ramsey* was about to enter the river. Five Greenpeace members, including Trevor, were charged with intent to obstruct a navigable river, which carries a possible penalty of imprisonment with hard labor for seven years.

> *We can't rest until our national government chooses the human race over the nuclear race.*
>
> —*Rev. Jesse Jackson*

* The first of three negotiating committees consisted of John Babkoff, Franklin Folsom, Carlos de la Fuente and Judith Rane. A second committee, Allan Affeldt and Carlos de la Fuente, continued negotiations. Allan Affeldt, Rhoda Evans and Joe Kinczel made up the third delegation. All are GPM veterans.

The summer of 1987 saw three major US marches which were direct spinoffs of the GPM. In Michigan a small number of people set out from Sault Ste. Marie on May 31. For the next two months they were joined by scores of others and fed by churches as they passed through communities along the route. Weekends found the greatest number on the road, as working people came out on their free time to support the cause. Corinne Carey, an organizer for the march through Michigan, had been working on a feeder march which was to have joined the GPM in 1986. "We had to commit ourselves the week PRO-Peace collapsed, so we shelved the idea until this year," Corinne said. "We drew very much on our GPM experience to set this [Michigan march] up." The march through Michigan ended in Detroit on August 9, the anniversary of the bombing of Nagasaki.

Two groups of walkers, inspired by the GPM, made their way through New England in August, joining forces on September 7 in Groton, Connecticut, where they staged a demonstration against the Electric Boat Company, manufacturer of nuclear submarines.

Supporting these three marches, as well as the Florida action, was a small group of GPM veterans called Seeds of Peace. (For address see appendix.) At the conclusion of the Great Peace March, the Seeds people raised money and bought some of the March vehicles, refurbished them, and made themselves and the vehicles available for support of peace actions planned by others. Despite financial struggles, the group continues, at this writing, to operate as a support team.

The idea of regional marches grew elsewhere. Day-long or weekend-long marches have been held in many areas around the United States since the conclusion of the GPM. The Peace March of Southern California, formed after the March ended, holds a monthly walk somewhere in Southern California.

Coleen Ashly, Mordecai Roth, B.J. King-Taylor, Katea Golub and others active in the Southern California group formed a nation-wide network for 1988 State Peace Marches, an ambitious effort to have simultaneous grassroots marches in nearly every state, aimed at informing voters about peace and weapons issues in the presidential election year.

For the most part, local peace organizations tend to be geo-

If we can agree that our objective is not marching but mobilizing, we must show how we can mobilize through our marching.

–Allan Affeldt, Marcher

175

graphically tethered to the communities where their membership lives and works. They are a part of the peace movement that does not usually move. But the March projected something new onto the political and social scene. In a very real sense, it brought the peace movement to the people. By its presence, there was peace activity where there had often been none before. And where there had been peace activity, the GPM's passage increased its intensity and the character of personal involvement. Regional marches have been expanding that influence.

Communities that reacted to the news of the impending arrival of the March with everything from passivity to skepticism to fear, were in almost every case turned around by the time the March left. From what I (C.F.) was able to gather, it was usually the friendliness and human decency of the Marchers and the cleanup campaign—that always left neighborhoods or communities neater than when we arrived—that caused folks to see the Marchers in a different light. The impression was distinct and almost universally positive. In many towns where we stayed, the peace movement came to have a better name than it had before the GPM passed through.

Having the March in a community often paved the way for subsequent events that might not otherwise have taken place. Audry Jump, a friendly Presbyterian woman in her 70s, felt that this was true in Cedar City, Utah. In a Christmas letter she wrote to friends and family in 1987 she said, "In spite of the turmoil in the world, we have been very much encouraged by events that have happened here locally—like the visit of the Soviet and American gymnastic teams who put on a beautiful, non-competitive exhibition here at our local college. The community gave them a royal reception at the airport, streets lined with citizens waving both nations' flags as they rode into town, a gala parade down Main Street and all kinds of loving, accepting feelings going on for a whole week. The media did a wonderful job of reporting stories of friendship between Soviets and Americans. It was a strong message to each of our governments. We are sure the Great Peace March which came through Cedar City in '86 helped pave the way for this good experience."

Like the people in Cedar City and the man who dared to write about the March to his local newspaper, many former Marchers and supporters feel that to be against nuclear weapons is to be mainstream.

Jamie Stewart, a 33-year-old activist in St. George, Utah, started a petition drive in her community early in 1987. The petition with 800 signatures was sent to Utah Senator Jake Garn asking for a decrease in funding for nuclear weapons testing and an increase in funding for the National Institutes of Health. "I think the March set the tone and the stage for the petition drive," said Jamie. "The petition was the first [such] statement St. George ever made. Eight hundred signatures may not seem like much, but it is fantastic for a community like St. George."

"Peace the 31st: A Day of World Healing," a cooperative event held at the same hour worldwide on December 31, 1986, and again in 1987, brought together millions of people for an hour of prayer or meditation for peace in their local communities. Participating towns along the March route reported surprisingly large gatherings which organizers attributed to the influence of the GPM.

This influence was not easily achieved. The relationship of PRO-Peace with nationally established peace organizations had been clouded from the beginning. In 1985, PRO-Peace sent a letter outlining plans for the March to peace groups across the country. This letter offended many who received it. The National Committee on the Freeze barely passed a resolution supporting the March in 1985, and other groups were openly critical of Mixner and distanced themselves from him. Susan Keene, a Salt Lake City Quaker, summed up the feeling of many: "We felt the attitude of PRO-Peace was that all the peace groups should send all their money to them and let them do this big media thing with celebrities. We said, 'To heck with them.'"

Other organizations echoed this attitude. To some of them, the PRO-Peace project seemed a mischievous, even dangerous diversion of funds and energy from serious work for peace. Once the March was on the road, however, most who had initially opposed the idea realized that the failure of the March would have negative repercussions throughout the peace community. Meg Gage, executive director of the Peace Development Fund, said, "As much as I wasn't in favor of [PRO-Peace's March], it must not fail. The failure would be bigger than the March, and we can't afford this right now."

Although the Peace Development Fund was the only peace organization that backed the post-Barstow GPM with a substantial financial contribution, the logistic support of numerous peace

On average it costs about the same to launch the latest nuclear missile submarine as it does to build 450,000 homes.

–Council on Economic Priorities

177

groups across the country was certainly a factor in its eventual success. But it was far from a one-way street. Most of the groups that provided help have realized considerable benefits, too. *

Marchers swelled the ranks of protesters at the Nevada Test Site from the earliest days of the GPM. The crowds at demonstrations there mushroomed in 1987, with the Mother's Day action in May, 1987, drawing 3,000 demonstrators, many of them GPM veterans. Working with American Peace Test to organize the event were several Marchers, and they and others from the March continued to play an important role at most test site demonstrations.

The nuclear bomb says to us: "Make peace or perish!"

–Peace Pilgrim

Other peace groups as well benefited from cooperation with the GPM. People in the Greater Cleveland Freeze office were aware in October, 1985, that the PRO-Peace sponsored march would be in Cleveland at the same time as their annual Freeze Walk. "We saw it as a threat and an opportunity," recalled Mick Latkovich, director of development. "The question was whether we could work something out cooperatively with the March. It didn't look as if we could with Mixner." When PRO-Peace failed, the Freeze office continued to work toward a joint walk, and the months of planning paid off. (See Chapter VI.) "We got a tremendous boost in numbers, and we got very good media coverage," continued Mick. "Our membership numbers have grown tremendously since. It has been partly due to the March and partly because our methods have gotten better."

In many areas it was the local peace organizations that did much of the pre-planning and site procurement so vital to the daily operation of the March. The sometimes urgent necessity for this kind of help was a unifying and vitalizing influence for many groups. Joe Ruhlman, a Nebraskan for Peace from North Platte, said, "The March forced us to quickly muster up whatever resources we had. It was something tangible we could do. The cohesion of the group has grown steadily since then. We've added members and grown more active."

It was not only Nebraskans for Peace and Greater Cleveland Freeze that reported significant gains in membership after involvement with the GPM. Peace organizations in Philadelphia, Omaha, Lincoln, Denver, Des Moines and Iowa City all reported growth.

---

* One of the last decisions made by the GPM's Board of Directors was to turn over to the Peace Development Fund any money remaining at the conclusion of the March. After selling the GPM equipment, the corporation had a surplus. We were able to give $50,000 to the organization that helped the March stay alive in Barstow eight months earlier.

The March provided a fresh sense of hope to many nearly burned-out activists as well as inspiration for newcomers to the movement. Chris Lundholm, a member of the Peace and Action Express in Vail, Colorado, said, "The March gave those of us who had been active a sense of hopefulness. It energized us. It was exciting." And according to Ginny McGlaughlin, executive director of the Philadelphia Freeze Voter, "It turned people on. It put some life back into the Philadelphia Freeze. It also involved people who weren't involved before. I don't know what it did for the apathetic, but it was a catalyst for people looking for inspiration and motivation."

At the very moment the GPM arrived in Washington, the White House responded to overtures the March had made weeks before. From that contact a dialogue was initiated between Marchers and representatives of other peace organizations on the one hand, and representatives of the current administration on the other. Three such joint discussions were held in 1987, and the door remained open for further talks.

All the personal growth, all the efforts at peaceful community living, all the public education that took place on the Great Peace March, have generated hope and lifted the spirits of innumerable people. Beyond that, something has changed: popular opinion about the urgent need for nuclear disarmament has altered. Poll after poll shows that people generally share the goal of peace groups, both abroad and in the United States.

And there is evidence that political leaders can also respond to peace organizations. According to John Hersey, writing in *The New Yorker*[*], International Physicians for the Prevention of Nuclear War (IPPNW) decided on July 1, 1985, to make its central goal the achievement of a ban on the testing of nuclear weapons. Less than four weeks later, Mikhail Gorbachev announced that the Soviet Union would cease testing until the end of the year—and longer if the United States also stopped testing. As the end of 1985 approached, Dr. Bernard Lown, American co-chair of IPPNW, spent three hours with Gorbachev, urging him to extend the moratorium for at least three months. Very soon after this meeting, Gorbachev did extend it.

[*] *The New Yorker*, September 7, 1987

On average it costs about the same to arm and train one soldier as it does to educate 80 children.

–Council on Economic Priorities

Demonstrations at the Nevada Test Site in 1986 increased in intensity, but were not enough to persuade the administration to join the test ban. However, it seems fair to say that developements stemming from the kind of lobbying that Dr. Lown did—and from the ongoing demonstration which was the Great Peace March—have been part of a general increase in peace actions. These actions, in turn, have played a role in bringing about dramatic changes on the international scene.

Michio Kaku has pointed to this: "In spite of staggering odds against them, the people—the community of peace activists worldwide—have influenced and shaped US defense policy." They helped to bring about a situation which made possible the first treaty to abolish one whole class of nuclear weapons. And although this was not publicly acknowledged by the Reagan administration, credit to the work and influence of the peace movement was given by Soviet Chairman Mikhail Gorbachev during the Washington signing of the INF treaty.

Now, as the educational and mobilizing force of new marches, witnesses and actions extends the GPM experience, it seems realistic to look forward to other such treaties and finally to the removal of all nuclear weapons—one of the greatest achievements in history. It will be the result of the efforts and courage of many. But at the core, much of it can be credited to people who take charge of their lives and pull the world back from imminent self-destruction. It will be ordinary people, learning together and moving together toward an era in which human talents and the world's resources can more fully serve our human family.

The experience of success with the March gave me hope that we can be successful on a larger scale.

–Monica Green,
Co-Chair, SANE/FREEZE

Afterword

What Next?

Attempts to shut down Rocky Flats or the Nevada Test Site? These efforts go forward and expand, and I hope they succeed.

Citizen exchanges with the Soviet Union to increase understanding and friendship and trust? These too go forward, and I know from personal experience that they can bring important results.

Hundreds of other efforts are ongoing—and on-growing. May they all achieve their goal, which often is the essential one of consciousness raising.

Closing plants that make weapons or that test weapons may delay production. Such closings will definitely be good for increasing general awareness of the terrible danger we still face even after the INF Treaty goes into effect. Ninety-seven percent of the nuclear weapons are still out there, ready.

But the closing of facilities does not go for the jugular of the monster that will kill us if we don't kill it. It does not paralyze, or even greatly weaken, the military industrial complex. Factories and test facilities can move and set up in new locations.

The Association of Anti-Nuclear Archaeologists [January 16, 1988] announced that 1,315 archaeologists in Japan had signed an appeal for the elimination of nuclear weapons.

But there is one thing that will stop the arms race—that will immobolize the Great Destroyer. And what is that one thing? A stoppage of the funds that keep it in business.

All appropriations for nuclear weapons, indeed for all weapons, come from the House of Representatives. If we take actions that persuade Congress to conform to the popular will, there will be no more money for nuclear arms. If all funds dry up, SAC will very soon be unable to launch missiles that carry nuclear warheads. Trident submarines will be unable to put out to sea. The arms merchants will be out of business—unless they convert to producing things that the world desperately needs but is not getting because of the arms race. And Congress can guarantee a market for the necessities of life, just as it provides a market for the instruments of death. Furthermore, as economists have demonstrated, conversion to peacetime production will create many more jobs than now exist in the nuclear arms industry.

With the Soviets also stopping production of nuclear weapons—a step they are obviously eager to take—the arms race will come to a halt.

How can Congress be persuaded to cease taking the taxpayers' money and giving it to the nuclear industry?

This can be achieved if we defeat all candidates for Congress who have been voting for the recent insane military budgets. If hawks do survive the electoral process because people have not yet learned that their representatives are frustrating their desire for peace, then other measures are available.

Unending picketlines can be very persuasive, and they can persist wherever and whenever the hawks appear in their constituencies or in the capital. Sit-ins too, can be remarkably effective supplements to all other forms of lobbying, which must continue. Mikhail Gorbachev has put the matter very bluntly, not just for his compatriots but for all of us: "People cannot afford to waste time. It may be too late tomorrow, and the day after tomorrow may never come."

And what will we have to do to insure peace, day after tomorrow, if disarmament does come, as I think it will? That must be the subject of another book—and other marches.

Meanwhile, for the rich information she supplied about our March and for the immense labor she performed for our book on it, I thank Connie Fledderjohann. I also thank Gerda Lawrence for the detailed material that makes up Chapter IV, and I am indebted to Richard Polese for his additions to our information and for his many specific suggestions about the text. Finally I owe a special debt to Mary Elting Folsom who performed the difficult task of making a unified book out of the very different writings of three very different people.

Franklin Folsom

. . . . . .

Learning to Live Together

In looking back over my life on the March, as well as my work on this book, I have come to realize how many different perceptions there are of what most of us thought was the same event. That being so, an evaluation of those eight-and-a-half months should include a a word about my own experience.

The most difficult aspect of the GPM for me was admitting and dealing with my own intolerance. Living in Peace City meant living beside and working with people whom I would rarely, if ever, have encountered in my more conventional life. To listen to and find value in words coming from a barefoot "punk" teenager with a ring through her nose was not easy. But it was important.

If the world is to know lasting peace it's going to take more than getting rid of the bombs. We've got to learn to live side-by-side and talk together without insisting that our neighbors conform to our ideas of what is "right," whether the neighbor be the Marcher in the next tent, the family next door or the country half-way round the world. Peace City gave me the opportunity to discover the extent of my acceptance of individual differences as well as a chance to expand it. If Marchers had been only people with whom I felt comfortable I would have been denied an opportunity for growth.

In addition, the diversity of our population inspired hope in many who saw us. Had the GPM been a structured and disciplined group of like-minded individuals, we would have undoubtedly been more effective in communicating our overt message, and life in Peace City would have been easier, but the diversity that people found inspiring would have been missing. Several of those whom I interviewed said they were encouraged by the fact that we Peace City citizens could live, work and walk together despite our different lifestyles and backgrounds. "If you could do it, maybe there's hope for the world," one interviewee told me.

Finally, I was encouraged by the tolerance, understanding and love of many of my fellow Marchers. Despite the instances of pettiness, bickering and even chaos, there was always someone around who, by example or words, could restore hope in my heart. Those friends, and many like them, are out in the world now spreading the message of peace. Our community that was Peace City has dispersed around the country—and around the world. But the bond which united us remains. And wherever we meet, whether in twos or threes or large groups, the memories are rekindled, the stories retold and we know that somehow our world has changed.

Connie Fledderjohann

Appendices

Appendix A

The Great Peace March
by Carl Sagan *

Following is the complete text of the speech given by Carl Sagan on November 15, 1986. It was delivered to the Great Peace Marchers in Lafayette Park, across Pennsylvania Ave. from the White House:

Human beings come from a long nomadic tradition. For hundreds of thousands of years, before we invented cities, we were hunter/gatherers. We marched, often over long distances, to survive. I think the Great Peace March has tapped into that ancient tradition.

Another thing that has happened since a few hundred thousand years ago is that our technology has given us enormous powers both for good and for evil. And in the latter category the United States and the Soviet Union together have contaminated this planet with 60,000 nuclear weapons. Always done in the cause of national security. Always done because of some abuse on the other side. And since each side has committed a list of abuses as long as my arm, each side can always point to a reason for further escalation of the arms race. The circumstances now are that there are an obscene number of nuclear weapons on the planet, far more than are needed for any conceivable purpose, and certainly far more than are needed to dissuade the other side from doing something stupid.

The number of cities on the planet Earth, if you define a city as having 100,000 people or more, is only 2,300. The United States and the Soviet Union have a number of strategic weapons, that is, nuclear weapons attached to delivery systems which can carry them halfway across the planet, approaching 25,000. That means that if the United States and the Soviet Union wished to dedicate two nuclear weapons to every city on Earth, they could demolish every city on the planet and have almost 20,000 strategic weapons left over. These two nations also have some thirty to thirty-five thousand tactical nuclear weapons, most of which are more powerful than the bombs that destroyed Hiroshima and Nagasaki. This is madness! There is no reason to have such weapons in such numbers, even from the most narrow perspective of national security.

- *An Extraordinary Danger*

The prompt deaths from a major war between the United States and the Soviet Union are variously estimated as between a few hundred million people killed outright to an estimate by the World Health Organization of 2.2 billion people killed outright. Beyond that there are long-term effects from persistent radioactivity, from epidemics and pandemics associated with the lowering of resistance to disease and the destruction of hospitals and physicians, and then the long-term consequences of nuclear war called Nuclear Winter. The additional deaths from these longer-term causes are estimated again in the billions. If you kill one or two billion people outright and then you kill billions more through the longer-term consequences of nuclear war, you are approaching the total number of people on the planet, which is only about 5 billion people. **This is the first time in the history of the human species that we have had this capability of destroying the global civilization, and possibly the species itself. It calls for extraordinary measures. It calls for extraordinary dedication. This is not business as usual.**

● *Accidental Nuclear War*

We live in the time of **Chernobyl** and **Challenger,** which remind us that high technology—into which enormous amounts of national prestige have been invested—can nevertheless fail spectacularly. And the lesson is clear: that nuclear weapons systems are also vulnerable. In fact, they are probably more vulnerable because nuclear weapons systems, by and large, cannot be tested, except by having a trial nuclear war. And few people wish to do that. **Chernobyl** and **Challenger** could be tested, and they were. They failed, nevertheless.

This is also the century of Hitler and Stalin, a reminder that madmen can achieve the highest offices in modern industrial states.

You put these together and I think you see that there is a circumstance, perhaps not with us at the moment, but that sooner or later will come, when some concatenation of machine failure and human failure will result in a catastrophe of unprecedented proportions.

America has been slowly waking up to the fact that this administration has a more than passing acquaintance with incompetence and dishonesty. We who are concerned about the nuclear arms race have known about this for years. Maybe you can recall the comment of Mr. Reagan within the first year of his achieving office in which he said that ballistic missiles could be recalled in case you changed your mind after they were launched. Maybe you can recall that after an attempt to negotiate a proportional decline in the land-based arm of the nuclear triad with the Soviets, the President admitted that he had not realized that while the bulk of the Soviet strategic forces was land-based, the bulk of the U.S. forces was submarine based. This is the most elementary fact about the disposition of strategic forces. No one told him. No Secretary of Defense, no Secretary of State, no National Security Adviser, no Presidential Science Adviser, could tell the President this elementary fact.

Maybe you can also recall something called the window of vulnerability; the supposed vulnerability of the U.S. strategic forces to a massive Soviet attack. Maybe you can remember that those big boosters that supposedly caused the window of vulnerability were on the table at the meeting of Reagan and Gorbachev in Reykjavik and were not thrown away because the President had a passion for Star Wars.

● *Nuclear Testing*

As a clearer example, and a recent one, let's consider the issue of nuclear testing. On August 6, 1985, the 40th anniversary of the demolition of Hiroshima, the Soviet Union announced a unilateral moratorium on further underground nuclear testing. There is no claim that the Soviets cheated. There is excellent evidence that they abided by this self-imposed moratorium. But the American response has been contemptuous. Far from joining the Soviet moratorium, as the Soviets did in 1963 when the United States proposed a moratorium on above-ground tests, the United States has instead exploded some 25 nuclear weapons, one of which was exploded during a demonstration I participated in at the Nevada Nuclear Test Site.*

---

* The Soviet Union extended its unilateral moratorium several times, continually asking the United States to join them. Finally, the Soviet Union ended its moratorium on testing in February 1987 after the United States continued to test in 1987.

What is the reason that the United States doesn't join the moratorium? It is interesting to look at the excuses handed to us. First there was the claim that the Soviets were insincere, that they had done a "flurry" (that was the Administration's word) of testing just before they announced their moratorium. If you look at the Administration's own records of how many tests there were by the Soviets you find that in the first seven or eight months of 1985 there were nine Soviet weapons exploded; just the average for both nations for this period. There was no "flurry."

No, the Administration then said, that wasn't the reason. The reason was that the Soviets will never permit on-site verification. They might blow up a very little weapon, and we couldn't detect it with seismometers outside the Soviet Union. Then an American environmental organization, the Natural Resources Defense Council, made an arrangement with the Soviets, because of which there are American scientists and American seismometers in place at this moment at the Soviet test center in Semipalatinsk. So now we do not hear about Soviet reluctance about on-site verification.

The Administration has had to go on to other excuses. First of all, we are told, the Soviets might wait until there is a natural earthquake in Soviet Central Asia and then explode their nuclear weapons. Can you imagine the Soviet scientist with his finger on the button waiting for a natural earthquake? Then we are told the Soviets might do what's called decoupling. They might construct a large underground cavern, hang the nuclear weapons from the cavern and explode it so there would be a damped seismic wave. Yes, you can do that with small nuclear weapons, so small that it would have very little bearing on the nuclear test ban. But for big weapons you can't. And the excavation of the cavern would be detectable to satellite reconnaissance.

Then there is the excuse which really tops them all, and I'm sorry to say it is an excuse echoed even by the Chairman of the Joint Chiefs of Staff, namely that the Soviets will test on the other side of the Sun. I maintain that when the justification for continued U.S. testing reaches such a level, we can clearly see that the arguments are bankrupt.

There is a contention that further testing is necessary to keep the bombs "safe," just as we heard in the 1960's that we had to do further testing to keep the bombs "clean." There is more than a bit of irony in the idea of a "safe" nuclear weapon. In any case, those who constructed U.S. nuclear weapons have repeatedly testified that you do not have to blow up nuclear weapons in order to guarantee their safety. **So the Administration's argument reduces itself to the need to test nuclear weapons to develop further generations of nuclear weapons. I say that our highest priority should be to develop further generations of human beings, not future generations of nuclear weapons.**

- *Star Wars*

Let me say a word about Star Wars, because Star Wars is clearly one of the reasons why continuing U.S. nuclear testing is advocated by this administration. (If there were a moratorium on both sides on further nuclear weapons testing, then a major propellant for the continuing escalation of the arms race would be undone. While a moratorium isn't enough by itself—you would also have to reduce nuclear weapons—it is a very important and easily verifiable step, and therefore very important.) The Administration is pursuing what the President calls his "vision" of Star Wars. The idea, as the President and the Secretary of Defense repeatedly tell us, is to have a shield which would protect the civilian population of the United States against a Soviet attack.

The Administration's own technical people (who are not hostile to Star Wars, but people in favor of it), tell us that in some decades, if all goes well, after the expenditure of one or two trillion dollars, we might have a system which could shoot down 70 or 80 or 90 percent of

Soviet strategic warheads. If you shoot down 90 percent of them, guess what? Ten percent get through. Ten percent of 10,000 is one thousand strategic weapons. One thousand Soviet strategic weapons landing on American territory are enough to utterly destroy the United States as a functioning political entity and to kill tens of millions of Americans. This is the shield on behalf of which a historic agreement was thrown away in Reykjavik. What could the President be thinking of ?

We should also remember that one to two trillion dollars is an awful lot of money. For example, two trillion dollars is the national debt. The national debt. The one that all those people concerned for fiscal responsibility tell us about. Two **trillion** dollars, to be spent on a system which cannot accomplish its objective. What are we thinking of? By the way, it's an interesting question to ask, how much money has been spent on the cold war all in all by the United States? In constant 1977 dollars, by the time that this Administration leaves office, the United States will have spent 3.7 trillion dollars on the arms race. This is enough money to buy everything in the United States except the land—every house, every skyscraper, every automobile, every boat, every truck, every toy, every diaper, everything in the United States. This is what we have spent on the arms race. So I ask you, is this the most effective use of the national treasury?

● *The Responsibility is Ours*

It is easy to criticize President Reagan. And it is amazing that there has been so little of it since he is so worthy of criticism. But I think it's important not to be too hard on the President. We have much more responsibility than he has. We let this happen. We, all of us, including the press, did not speak out, did not criticize, did not effectively present alternatives and constructive points of view. Let us try to take such constructive attitudes to blaze a new trail for the United States.

What will it take? What peaceful, loving ways are available to cut through the denial and the self-propagating paranoia which drives the arms race? These Peace Marchers have just walked across the United States. They know the dangers of the nuclear arms race. They recognize its seriousness. They have embraced Albert Einstein's call for a new way of thinking. There are other people who have taken other actions. We heard from Charles Heyder, an astronomer who's fasting unto death because of this nuclear arms race. There are some of us who have committed non-violent civil disobedience at the Nevada Nuclear Test Site in another attempt to call attention to what must be done. There are people across the country who fully understand what is needed, and the dangers that the policies of this administration and previous administrations have put us in. But there are a group of extremists across the street who have not yet understood. It is our job to explain it to them.

No one says this is an easy job. It isn't easy because it involves a change in our way of thinking—for example, the idea that more nuclear weapons don't make you safer. This idea is in defiance of the conventional wisdom. **If you grow up in a place where there are snowball fights, you rapidly learn that the more snowballs you have, the safer you are. But the essential lesson for us is that nuclear weapons are not snowballs.** It's a hard lesson.

● *It Can Be Done*

It's difficult, but it can be done. The reason I say it can be done, and I am positive it can be done, is because we humans have done much more difficult things in the past. Let me remind you of just one, the institution of chattel slavery. The idea was that it was fitting and proper and just and even God-given that some human beings should own other human beings; that people were property; that you could own people lock, stock, barrel, spouse, and child. This was not a view of only a few evil people. This was the worldwide standard of belief.

Today we are embarrassed by it. We look back on it and wonder how our ancestors could have done it. But they did it, and not just a few people, not just a small slave-owning class, but the Church, and the political leaders, and the famous intellectuals and academics and scholars. (Aristotle, for example, believed that some people were naturally slaves and some people were naturally masters.) Today there is no more chattel slavery, or almost none, on the planet Earth. We have made a stirring worldwide change in our way of thinking on this issue.

The vested interests in slavery were far greater than the vested interests in continuing the nuclear arms race. Generals and presidents and Communist party leaders have children. They, too, have hopes for the future. They are vulnerable to the same appeals as we are. Reason ultimately will prevail because the alternative is simply that there would be no one left to do either reasoning or emoting.

I salute you, I welcome you, and I assure you that there is a change happening at this moment—changing opinion, new sorts of political action—and we are going to see a significant change in U.S. policy on nuclear weapons and on many other issues.

CAMPSITE ON POWER LINE ROAD
OUTSIDE BAKER CAL.

11:00 AM
THE MARCHERS
HAVE HAD
BREAKFAST AND
MOVED ON -
WORKERS
HOLD HANDS +
SHARE
STRENGTH

4-1-86

Guy Colwell 1986

Appendix B

Statement of Purpose

Following is the Statement of Purpose of the Great Peace March:

The Great Peace March for Global Nuclear Disarmament is an abolitionist movement. We believe that great social change comes about when the will of the people becomes focused on a moral imperative. By marching for nine months across the United States, we will create a non-violent focus for positive change; the imperative being that nuclear weapons are politically, socially, economically and morally unjustifiable, and that, in any number, they are unacceptable. It is the responsibility of a democratic government to implement the will of its people, and it is the will of the people of the United States and many other nations to end the nuclear arms race.

Our specific objectives are:

1. A verifiable Comprehensive Test Ban Treaty

2. No militarization of space

3. Enforcement by all governments of the Non-proliferation Treaty

4. Continuous, intensive negotiations between the United States and the USSR leading to agreements on nuclear weapons control

5. A 'No-First-Use' pledge by all the nuclear nations of the world

6. A verifiable global freeze on the testing, production, and deployment of all nuclear weapons, missiles and their delivery systems

7. A nuclear-weapon-free Europe and the Pacific

8. Reductions leading to the elimination of nuclear weapons stockpiles

9. Redirection of resources from nuclear weapons manufacture to socially useful fuller employment projects

10. Immediate action directed toward safe disposal of nuclear waste resulting from the manufacture of nuclear weapons

We walk together to call attention to a danger so serious and so urgent that we have given up our jobs and homes, our incomes and comforts for nine months to cross the United States. Our purpose is to educate and to demonstrate our conviction that there is hope and that each individual can make a difference. As citizens of the world it is our responsibility to our children, our planet, and ourselves to eliminate the danger of nuclear war.

We welcome and encourage representatives from peace and justice organizations throughout the world to join us in a dialogue of co-operation and education as an alternative to the rhetoric of confrontation.

We believe that by walking together we will be one step closer to a world free of nuclear weapons and a world free of war.

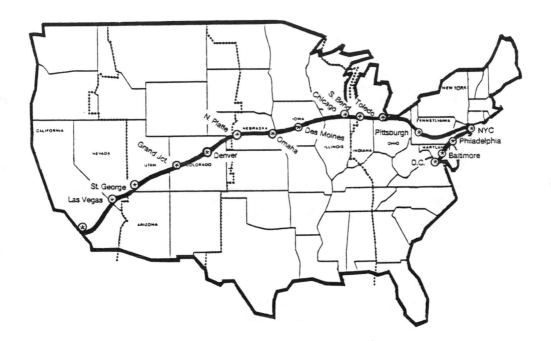

Appendix C

Itinerary

March 1	Los Angeles, CA	May 1	Manderfield, UT
March 2	Irwindale, CA	May 2-3	Cove Fort, UT
March 3	Claremont, CA	May 4-5	Cisco, UT
March 4	Chaffey College, CA	May 6	Rabbit Valley, CO
March 5-6	Glen Helen, CA	May 7	Loma, CO
March 7	Hesperia Lakes, CA	May 8-9	Grand Junction, CO
March 8-9	Victorville, CA	May 10	DeBeque, CO
March 10-15	Stoddard Wells Road	May 11	Parachute, CO
	near Barstow, CA	May 12	Rifle, CO
March 16-27	Barstow, CA	May 13	New Castle, CO
March 28	Yermo, CA	May 14-15	Glenwood Springs, CO
March 29	Bureau of Land Manage-	May 16	Eagle, CO
	ment Mojave Desert	May 17	Edwards, CO
	Site #1, CA	May 18-19	Vail, CO
March 30	B.L.M. site #2, CA	May 20	Copper Mountain, CO
March 31	B.L.M. site #3, CA	May 21	Keystone, CO
April 1	B.L.M. site #4, CA	May 22	Loveland Basin, CO
April 2-3	B.L.M. site #5, CA	May 23-25	Lawson, CO
April 4-7	Near Whiskey Pete's	May 26-27	Golden, CO
	Casino just west of	May 28	Red Rocks, CO
	CA/NV border	May 29-31	Denver, CO
April 8	B.L.M. site #6 near	June 1	Adams County, CO
	Jean, NV	June 2	Lochbuie, CO
April 9	B.L.M. site #7 near	June 3	Roggen, CO
	Sloan, NV	June 4	Wiggins, CO
April 10-11	West of Las Vegas, NV	June 5	Ft. Morgan, CO
April 12	Las Vegas, NV	June 6	Merino, CO
April 13	B.L.M. site #8 near	June 7-8	Sterling, CO
	Apex, NV	June 9	Proctor, CO
April 14	B.L.M. site #9	June 10	Sedgwick, CO
April 15	B.L.M. site #10	June 11	Big Springs, NE
April 16	B.L.M. site #11	June 12	Ogallala, NE
April 17-18	B.L.M. site #12	June 13	Paxton, NE
April 19	Mesquite, NV	June 14	Sutherland, NE
April 20	Littlefield, AZ	June 15-16	North Platte, NE
April 21	Shivwits Paiute Band	June 17	Brady, NE
	Reservation, UT	June 18	Willow Island, NE
April 22-23	St. George, UT	June 19	Lexington, NE
April 24	B.L.M. site #13	June 20	Elm Creek, NE
April 25	B.L.M. site #14	June 21	Kearney, NE
April 26	B.L.M. site #15	June 22	Shelton, NE
April 27	Summit, UT	June 23-24	Grand Island, NE
April 28	Panguitch, UT	June 25	Aurora, NE
April 29-30	Beaver, UT	June 26	York, NE

June 27	Tamora, NE
June 28	Seward, NE
June 29-30	Lincoln, NE
July 1	Ashland, NE
July 2	Papillion, NE
July 3-6	Council Bluffs, IA
July 7	Treynor, IA
July 8	Oakland, IA
July 9	Lewis, IA
July 10-11	Lake Anita, IA
July 12	Adair, IA
July 13	Stuart, IA
July 14	Earlham, IA
July 15	Adel, IA
July 16-17	Urbandale, IA
July 18	Des Moines, IA
July 19	Mitchellville, IA
July 20	Newton, IA
July 21	Grinnell, IA
July 22	Brooklyn, IA
July 23	Ladora, IA
July 24	South Amana, IA
July 25	Oxford, IA
July 26-27	Coralville, IA
July 28	West Branch, IA
July 29	Wilton, IA
July 30	Walcott, IA
July 31	Davenport, IA
August 1-2	East Moline, IL
August 3	Hillsdale, IL
August 4	Prophetstown, IL
August 5	Sterling, IL
August 6	Dixon, IL
August 7	Amboy, IL
August 8	Shabbona, IL
August 9-10	Big Rock, IL
August 11	Aurora, IL
August 12	Lisle, IL
August 13	LaGrange, IL
August 14-17	Chicago, IL
August 18	Hammond, IN
August 19	Gary, IN
August 20	Indiana Dunes State Park, IN
August 21	LaPorte, IN
August 22	New Carlisle, IN
August 23-24	South Bend, IN
August 25	Elkhart, IN
August 26	Bristol, IN
August 27	Shipshewana, IN
August 28	Lagrange, IN
August 29	Angola, IN
August 30	Columbia, OH
Aug. 31-Sept. 1	Montpelier, OH
September 2	Wauseon, OH
September 3	Swanton, OH
September 4-5	Maumee, OH
September 6	Oregon, OH

September 7-8	Port Clinton, OH
September 9	Huron, OH
September 10	Vermillion, OH
September 11	Avon Lake, OH
September 12-14	Cleveland, OH
September 15	North Randall, OH
September 16	Aurora, OH
September 17	Garrettsville, OH
September 18	Warren, OH
September 19-20	Youngstown, OH
September 21	Petersburg, OH
September 22	Beaver Falls, PA
September 23	Economy, PA
September 24	Allegheny County, PA
September 25-26	Pittsburgh, PA
September 27	McKeesport, PA
September 28	Greensburg, PA
September 29	Ligonier, PA
September 30	Jennerstown, PA
October 1	Reels Center, PA
October 2-3	Bedford, PA
October 4	Breezewood, PA
October 5	McConellsburg, PA
October 6	St. Thomas, PA
October 7	Shippensburg, PA
October 8	Carlisle, PA
October 9-10	Harrisburg, PA
October 11	Hershey, PA
October 12	Lebanon, PA
October 13	Robesonia, PA
October 14	Reading, PA
October 15	Kutztown, PA
October 16-17	Allentown, PA
October 18	Phillipsburg, NJ
October 19	Anderson, NJ
October 20	Dover, NJ
October 21	Caldwell, NJ
October 22	Leonia, NJ
October 23-25	Manhattan, NY
October 26-27	Staten Island, NY
October 28	Rahway, NJ
October 29	New Brunswick, NJ
October 30	Princeton, NJ
October 31	Newton, PA
November 1	North Philadelphia, PA
November 2-3	Philadelphia, PA
November 4	Swarthmore, PA
November 5	New Castle, DE
November 6	Fair Hill, MD
November 7	Susquehana, MD
November 8	Hickory, MD
November 9	Perry Hall, MD
November 10-11	Baltimore, MD
November 12	Elkridge, MD
November 13	Beltsville, MD
November 14	Washington, D.C.
November 15	Washington, D.C.

Appendix D

Addresses of Spinoff Organizations

Many individual Marchers and groups of Marchers have been engaged in related follow-up activities since the end of the GPM. The addresses listed below are for organizations referred to in the text. Other Marcher organizations undoubtedly exist, but at the time of the writing the following ones were known to us:

International Peace Walk: P.O. Box 53412, Washington, D.C. 20009,
    Phone: 202/232-7055

1988 State March Project: 7250 Franklin Ave. #112 Los Angeles, CA 90048,
    Phone: 218/851-4931

Peacemaker Pen Pals: Mary Edwards, 227 No. Alarcon, Prescott, AZ 86301,
    Phone 602/778-9335

Peace March of Southern California: P.O. Box 3453, Granada Hills, CA 91344,
    Phone: 818/366-3234

Seeds of Peace: 1100 7th St. Suite. 1000, Washington, D.C. 20036,
    Phone: 202/466-2561

Shut Down: 1738 Pearl St., Boulder, CO 80302,
    Phone: 303/443-2822

Take Action!: c/o CALS, 454 Willamette St., Eugene, OR 97401

The Silver Thread Update: Bill O'Neill, 26 Huckins Neck Rd., Centerville, MA 02632

197

gear pile at the Payute Reservation, Utah

Appendix E

Congratulations from Senators

Senator Tom Harkin read the following proclamation at a rally in Washington on November 15, 1986:

United States Senate
Washington, D.C. 20510
November 15, 1986

Dear Peace Marchers:

Your long journey is finally over and congratulations are in order. What you have done demonstrates strength and conviction of a magnitude rarely seen for a cause that demands such efforts.

Stopping the nuclear arms race is a moral imperative shared by all citizens of the world. You have taken it upon yourselves to take this cause, the cause of peace, directly to all citizens of this nation, and through your actions to all citizens of the world. What you have done was not easy, your sacrifices were personal, though your goals were not. Actions such as these are inspiring, and what you stand for embodies the best of the American people.

We offer to you our heartfelt congratulations and support for your cause, the cause of all people everywhere: ending the nuclear arms race.

Sincerely,

Tom Harkin	John F. Kerry
Donald W. Riegle, Jr.	Paul Simon
Lowell P. Weicker, Jr.	Patrick J. Leahy
Claiborne Pell	Howard M. Metzenbaum
Edward M. Kennedy	Alan Cranston
Mark O. Hatfield	John Melcher
Spark M. Matsunaga	Carl Levin

Rebecca Knotting Bracelets

Guy Colwell 1986

Appendix F

Statement on Violence

While the March, which was deeply committed to nonviolence, moved across the country, leading behavioral scientists from around the world met in Spain under the auspices of the Spanish Committee of UNESCO. There they adopted the following statement which was later endorsed by the American Psychological Association and many other scientific groups:

Believing that is our responsibility to address from our particular disciplines the most dangerous and destructive activities of our speices, violence and war; recognizing that science is a human cultural product which cannot be definitive or all-encompassing; and gratefully acknowledging the support of the authroities of Seville and representatives of the Spanish UNESCO; we, the undersigned scholars from around the world and from relevant sciences, have met and arrived at the following Statement on Violence. In it, we challenge a number of biological findings that have been used, even by some in our disciplines, to justify violence and war. Because the alleged findings have contributed to an atmosphere of pessimism in our time, we submit that the open, considered rejection of these mis-statements can contribute significantly to the International Year of Peace.

Misuse of scientific theories and data to justify violence and war is not new but has been made since the advent of modern science. For example, the theory of evolution has been used to justify not only war, but also genocide, colonialism, and suppression of the weak.

We state our position in the form of five propositions. We are aware that there are many other issues about violence and war that could be fruitfully addressed from the standpoint of our disciplines, but we restrict ourselves here to what we consider a most important first step.

IT IS SCIENTIFICALLY INCORRECT to say that we have inherited a tendency to make war from our animal ancestors. Although fighting occurs widely throughout animal species, only a few cases of destructive intra-species fighting between organized groups have ever been reported among naturally living species, and none of these involve the use of tools designed to be weapons. Normal predatory feeding upon other species cannot be equated with intra-species violence. Warfare is a peculiarly human phenomenon and does not occur in other animals.

The fact that warfare has changed so radically over time indicates that it is a product of culture. Its biological connection is primarily through language which makes possible the coordination of groups, the transmission of technology, and the use of tools. War is biologically possible, but it is not inevitable, as evidenced by its variation in occurrence and nature over time and space. There are cultures which have not engaged in war for centuries, and there are cultures which have engaged in war frequently at some times and not at others.

IT IS SCIENTIFICALLY INCORRECT to say that war or any other violent behavior is genetically programmed into our human nature. While genes are involved at all levels of nervous system function, they provide a developmental potential that can be actualized only in conjunction with the ecological and social environment. While individuals vary in their predispositions to be affected by their experience, it is the interaction between their genetic endowment and conditions of nurturance that determines their personalities. Except for rare pathologies the genes do not produce individuals necessarily predisposed to violence. Neither

do they determine the opposite. While genes are co-involved in establishing our behavioral capacities, they do not by themselves specify the outcome.

IT IS SCIENTIFICALLY INCORRECT to say that in the course of human evolution there has been a selection for aggressive behavior more than for other kinds of behavior. In all well-studied species, status within the group is achieved by the ability to cooperate and to fulfill social functions relevant to the structure of that group. "Dominance" involves social bondings and affiliations; it is not simply a matter of the possession and use of superior physical power, although it does involve agressive behaviors. Where genetic selection for aggressive behavior has been artificially instituted in animals, it has rapidly succeeded in producing hyper-aggressive individuals; this indicates that aggression was not maximally selected under natural conditions. When such experimentally-created hyper-aggressive animals are present in a social group, they either disrupt its social structure or are driven out. Violence is neither in our evolutionary legacy nor in our genes.

IT IS SCIENTIFICALLY INCORRECT to say that humans have a "violent brain." While we do have the neural apparatus to act violently, it is not automatically activated by internal or external stimuli. Like higher primates and unlike other animals, our higher neural processes filter such stimuli before they can be acted upon. How we act is shaped by how we have been conditioned and socialized. There is nothing in our neurophysiology that compels us to react violently.

IT IS SCIENTIFICALLY INCORRECT to say that war is caused by "instinct" or any single motivation. The emergence of modern warfare has been a journey from the primacy of emotional and motivational factors, sometimes called "instincts," to the primacy of cognitive factors. Modern war involved institutional use of personal characteristics such as obedience, suggestibility, and idealism, social skills such as language, and rational considerations such as cost-calculation, planning, and information processing. The technology of modern war has exaggerated traits associated with violence both in the training of actual combatants and in the preparation of support for war in the general population. As a result of this exaggeration, such traits are often mistaken to be the causes rather than the consequences of the process.

We conclude that biology does not condemn humanity to war, and that humanity can be freed from the bondage of biological pessimism and empowered with confidence to undertake the transformative tasks needed in this International Year of Peace and in the years to come. Although these tasks are mainly institutional and collective, they also rest upon the consciousness of individual participants for whom pessimism and optimism are crucial factors. Just as "wars begin in the minds of men," peace also begins in our minds. The same species who invented war is capable of inventing peace.   The responsibility lies with each of us.

Seville, May 16, 1986

David Adams, Psychology, Wesleyan University, Middletown (CT) USA

S.A. Barnett, Ethology, The Australian National University, Canberra, Australia

N.P. Bechtereva, Neurophysiology, Institute for Experimental Medicine of Academy of Medical Sciences of USSR, Leningrad, USSR

Bonnie Frank Carter, Psychology, Albert Einstein Medical Center, Philadelphia (PA) USA

Jose M. Rodriguez Delgado, Neurophysiology, Centro de Estudios Neurobiologicos, Madrid, Spain

Jose Luis Diaz, Ethology, Instituto Mexicano de Psiquiatria, Mexico D.F. Mexico

Andrzej Eliasz, Individual Differences Psychology, Polish Academy of Sciences, Warsaw, Poland

Santiago Genoves, Biological Anthropology, Institute de Estudios Anthropologicos, Mexico D.F., Mexico

Benson E. Ginsburg, Behavior Genetics, University of Connecticut, Storrs (CT) USA

Jo Groebel, Social Psychology, Erziehungswissenschaftliche Hochschule, Landau, Federal Republic of Germany

Samir-Kumar Ghosh, Sociology, Indian Institute of Human Sciences, Calcutta, India

Robert Hinde, Animal Behavior, Cambridge University, UK

Richard E. Leakey, Physical Anthropology, National Museums of Kenya, Nairobi, Kenya

Taha H. Malasi, Psychiatry, Kuwait University, Kuwait

J. Martin Ramirez, Psychobiology, Universidad de Sevilla, Spain

Federico Mayor Zarogoza, Biochemistry, Universidad Autonoma, Madrid, Spain

Diana L. Mendoza, Ethology, Universidad de Sevilla, Spain

Ashis Nandy, Political Psychology, Center for the Study of Developing Societies, Delhi, India

John Paul Scott, Animal Behavior, Bowling Green State University, Bowling Green (OH) USA

Riitta Wahlstrom, Psychology, University of Jyvaskyla, Finland

ORANGE TOWN
ELECTION
WENSDAY MARCH 12 1986

SUNNY MORNING

WPatten
8 MILES OUTSIDE
BARSOA CACIE

LOVELAND PASS

SONGS & TEARS
THIS LAND WAS
MADE FOR YOU AND ME

W Mallon
May 21, 1986

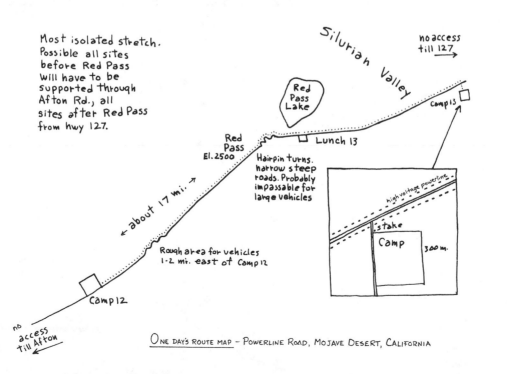

Most isolated stretch.
Possible all sites
before Red Pass
will have to be
supported through
Afton Rd., all
sites after Red Pass
from hwy 127.

Siluriah Valley

no access
till 127

Red
Pass
Lake

Lunch 13

Camp 13

Red
Pass
El. 2500

Hairpin turns.
narrow steep
roads. Probably
impassable for
large vehicles

high voltage powerline

stake

Camp   300 m.

about 17 mi.

Rough area for vehicles
1-2 mi. east of Camp 12

Camp 12

no
access
till Afton

ONE DAY'S ROUTE MAP – POWERLINE ROAD, MOJAVE DESERT, CALIFORNIA

Appendix G

A Selected Bibliography

● Following are a few of the major magazine articles written about the Great Peace March during the event. Articles appeared in hundreds of newspapers across the country, many of which were collected by Chris Ball of the GPM's Media department. Excellent continuing newspaper coverage of the GPM was given in feature stories by Kathleen Hendrix in the *Los Angeles Times*. *Peoples' Daily World* gave very full coverage from Cleveland to Washington.

Cooper, Marc. "PRO-Peace: Anatomy of a Failure." *L.A. Weekly*, March 21, 1986, p.4.

Gomez, Linda. "Putting Their Cause on the Line." *Life Magazine*, The Year in Pictures 1986, January 1987, p. 90.

Haferd, Laura. "A Day in the Life of the Great Peace March." *Akron Beacon Journal*, Sept. 14, 1986.

Kaplan, Marshall. "The Great Peace March for Global Nuclear Disarmament." *Fellowship Magazine*, December 1986, p. 15.

Kurek, Ellen. "The Great Peace March." *New Frontier*, October 1986, p. 33.

Kyle, Cynthia. "Peace Marchers Keep Up the Peace." *U.S. News and World Report*, Oct. 6, 1986, p. 25.

Lindeman, Les. "The Long Road to Lasting Peace." *50 Plus*, October, 1986, p. 22.

Sager, Mike. "Peace Comes to Washington: Marching to Save the World." *The Washington Post Magazine*, November. 9, 1986. p. 22.

Share, Jeff (photographs). "A Quixotic Quest for Peace." *People* magazine, October 27, 1986, p. 32.

Wadler, Joyce. "Feet Across America." *Daily News Magazine*, New York, October 19, 1986, p. 36. (Photos by Donal F. Holway.)

● Three books were read and referred to frequently by many Marchers throughout the nine-month life of Peace City. Because they may be helpful in understanding the character of the GPM they are included here:

Caldicott, Helen. *Missile Envy: The Arms Race and Nuclear War*. William Morrow, New York, 1984 (Bantam Books edition, 1985.)

Keyes, Ken. *The Hundredth Monkey: There Is No Cure for Nuclear War, Only Prevention*. Vision Books, 790 Commercial Ave., Coos Bay, Oregon, 1982.

Pilgrim, Peace. *Peace Pilgrim: Her Life and Work in Her Own Words*. Ocean Tree Books, P.O. Box 1295, Santa Fe, New Mexico, 1982.

● Many Marchers themselves have had the urge to write and publish, both during and after the March. Here are some of the books and booklets which have appeared in print or will soon be published:

A Peace Offering: From The Great Peace March to the Mississippi Peace Cruise. The Great Peace March, July, 1986. (Bilingual text in English and Russian.)

Atlee, Tom. *Great Peace March Update*, and *You Ain't Seen Nothin' Yet: A Marcher Networking Book* (with Karen Mercer). The Great Peace March, 1986. (The first appeared periodically during the March and was sent to people supporting the GPM; the latter was given to Marchers departing at Washington and contained information about individual Marchers' interests.)

Boggs, Lesha (ed.). *The Silver Thread Directory.* The Great Peace March for Global Nuclear Disarmament, 1986. (Over 700 individual photos of Marchers, with addresses and other March memorabilia—considered the "yearbook" of the GPM. *Silver Thread Updates*, including address changes and other Marcher news, are published periodically by Bill O'Neill, 26 Huckins Neck Road, Centerville, MA 02632.)

Butler, Ashley. *Never Turning Back.* (copyrighted manuscript)

Gonzalez, Sharon, and Roberta Wilson. *Personal Disarmament: Lessons of the Great Peace March.* (copyrighted manuscript)

Johnson, Tom (ed.) *Walking as a Metaphor for Peace.* The Great Peace March, 1986. With photographs by K.D. Kidder and Jeff Share. Sponsored by the Una Hanson Peace and Human Environment Foundation, Salt Lake City, Utah.

Krieger, Michael. *As the Train Rolls By.* Peace City Press, P.O. Box 100, Hollywood, CA, 90068, 1987. (poetry)

Macfarlane, Anne. *Feet Across America.* New Women's Press, P.O. Box 47-339, Auckland, New Zealand, 1987.

Sahlem, Frank. *Road Poems.* Frank Sahlem, publisher, 833 Fifth St. #307, Santa Monica, CA 1987.

Share, Jeff, and Kathleen Hendrix. *Routes of Peace: The Great Peace March and the American-Soviet Walk.* (in press)

Sickler, Martin. (untitled manuscript by a Marcher known as Born Again Hippie)

Zheutlin, Cathy. *Just One Step.* A Cathy Zheutlin Film, 8489 West Third Street #53, Los Angeles, 1988. (Feature length documentary.)

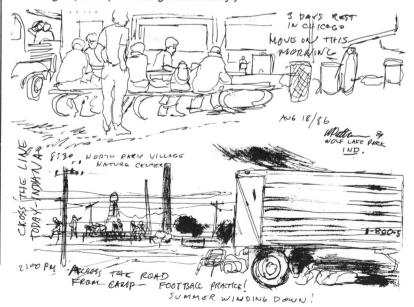

Acknowledgements

We offer our warmest thanks to these Marchers:

Guy Colwell, for permission to reproduce his drawings which appear in the appendices.

Daniel Coogan for permission to reproduce his photographs which appear on the cover and on pages 17, 21, 38, 54, 59, 62, 72, 73, 104, 118, 122, 124, 130, 142, 154, 155, 160.

William Patterson for permission to reproduce his drawings which appear in the appendices.

Jeff Share for permission to reproduce his photographs which appear on pages i, 21, 33, 52, 55, 80, 113, 114, 127, 129, 138, 145.

Ben Taslitz for permission to reproduce his photographs which appear on pages 58, 87, 99, 121, 141.

For giving us advice or information which helped us to shape this book we extend sincere thanks to Coleen Ashly, Tracy Bartlett, Buffy Boesen, Joseph Broido, Daniel Chavez, Walter Cobb, Evan Conroy, Mehi Cramer, Steven Kanner, Gerda Lawrence, Billy Lieb, David Miller, Bill O'Neill, Judith Rane, John Records, Rollin and Martha Rothhaar, Ralph Vrana, Dan Weinshenker, Sarah Willner, Jennifer York, Cathy Zheutlin and all the people interviewed by Connie Fledderjohann and Gerda Lawrence who gave us permission to quote them.

For providing a home for me (C.F.) while working on the book my thanks go to Diane Deschanel and Alan and Tessa Davis of Boulder. And for the use of their printer, thanks to the Rocky Mountain Peace Center.

For patient and creative work on this book we thank Michael Krell of Desktop Personal Publishing, Boulder, Colorado.

For financial help that made this book possible we want to thank:

Irving Adler	J. Walter and Charlotte E. Cobb
Frank C. Allen	Kate Coyle
Howard and Mary Allen	Nancy Larrick Crosby
David Alman	Sue Daniels
Barbara Ashley	Tessa and Alan Davis
Elizabeth Bacon	Ann Deschanel
Elizabeth Bensen	Christopher DiSantis
Bebie Berg	Rosemary Doar
Joan Bockelmann	Kate Drew-Wilkinson
Buffy Boesen	James E. Dugan
Joan Bokaer	Evelyn C. Eckert
Phyllis Braiotta	Abraham Edel
Rachel G. Brown	Ann and Richard Edelman
Janet Buchan	Mary C. Edmonston
Ashley Butler	Jean Faivus
Helen M. Carroll	Marjorie Farmer
William V. Carter	Aileen Fisher
Jacques and Gerry Cartier	Marie Fay

Dirk Fledderjohann
Fred G. Folsom
Michael Folsom
Rachael Folsom
Dudley Foot
Sarah F. Foot
John B. Foster
Abby Fountain
Joseph Friendly
Maureen Gaffey
H.D. Gale
John H. Gaylord
Robert D. Goff
Irving E. and Esther Z. Goldberg
Paul Grotz
Julia Gosztylia
Olga Gow
Michael Hall
Suzanne Hamilton
Ann Hayes
June Hemmingson
Neil Hendricks
Sam Herman
Holly Hock
Boyer and Pat Jarvis
Tom and Gayle Joliet
Gloria Joy
Howard and Audrey Jump
Eric and Gay Johnson
Florence and Herbert Johnson
Rebecca Kanner
Susan Keller and Myron Shapero
Pard M.J. Keyser and
Catherine Keyser-Mary
Yvonne D. King
Casey Kraft
Chester F. Kupiec
Corliss Lamont
Gerda Lawrence
Jacquelyn and Russ Leckband
Emmy Lerma
John C. MacDonald
Lynne McGee
Ann McGovern
Alice S. McKenna
Sylvia McNair
Pearl and Karl W. Meissner
Paul and Vivian Merker
Maureen L. Mitchell
David Moérbe
Anna H. Morgan
Lloyd and Norma Morris
Robert and Diana Mueller
Mary P. Murray
Lynn Nadeau
Kouji and Mary Nakata

Stephanie Nichols
Beatrice Novobilski
Edie O'Donnell
Barbara and Mike Oshin
Kate Oser
The Peace Development Fund
Gerhard H. Pesman
Carolyn McClintock Peter
Robert W. Phares
Charlotte Phillips
John and Emily Powers
Bob Powne and Lorraine Heller
Lilian Moore Reavin
L. Willard Reynolds
Chandos and Theodore Rice
Mary Frances Rimerman
Oliver Roberts
Milly Basser Salwen
Carol Saunders
Michael Schwab
Fred Segal
Dixie Searway
Lori Shields
Ruth and Ralph Shikes
Mary Shoemaker
Irene Shonle
Guthrie Sillman
Betty Skipp
Hallett D. and
Mary Elizabeth Smith
Muriel and Joseph Spanier
Joseph R. and Lucy S. Still
Bianca Storlazzi
Lynnda Strong
Edith and Dick Sullwold
Brian Szittai
Mauricio Terrazas
Ed Trunck
Philip Vance
Aleida VanDyke
Lana Vining
Timothy and Diane Wagner
A. Gayle Waldrop
Patricia Waldrop
Eunice White
Gilbert and Anne White
Joan and Irving White
Theodore and Ruth Wilson
Sam Wolfe
Elizabeth Woods
Martha D. Wray
Kate Wylie
Paul Ziegler
Mirah Zeitlyn
Lore Zeller